Vintage Views

of Leelanau County

M. Christine Byron and Thomas R. Wilson

Sleeping Bear Press

Front Cover Illustration
View of Glen Lake from Sleeping Bear Dunes, 1938
Grand Rapids Public Library, Local Historical Collections
Hand-colored by Dianne Carroll-Burdick

Back Cover Illustration
Grand Rapids Public Library, Local Historical Collections

. . . .

Sleeping Bear Press
310 North Main Street
P.O. Box 20
Chelsea, MI 48118
www.sleepingbearpress.com

Printed and bound in Canada.

10 9 8 7 6 5 4 3 2 1

Library of Congress Cataloging-in-Publication Data
Byron, M. Christine, 1949-
Vintage views of Leelanau County / by M. Christine Byron and Thomas R. Wilson.
p. cm.
ISBN 1-58536-085-6
1. Leelanau County (Mich.)—History—Pictorial works. 2. Leelanau County
(Mich.)—History—Sources. I. Wilson, Thomas R., 1949- II. Title.

F572.L45 B97 2002
977.4'635—dc21
2002018762

Acknowledgments

Thanks to the writers of yesteryear for their glowing descriptions and praises of Leelanau County. Special thanks to Alan Campbell of the *Leelanau Enterprise* and Ken Hall of the *Traverse City Record Eagle* for their kind permission to use historical writings from their newspapers.

For their time, knowledge, and resources we extend special thanks to Laura Quackenbush of the Leelanau Historical Museum, Dave Taghon of the Empire Area Museum, Steve Harold of the Grand Traverse Pioneer and Historical Society, Mark Harvey of the State Archives of Michigan, Kim Mann of Sleeping Bear Dunes National Lakeshore, and Doris Brammer of the Glen Arbor History Group. Many institutions gave us permission to use their material, including the Bentley Historical Library at the University of Michigan, Local Historical Collections at the Grand Rapids Public Library, the Grand Traverse Lighthouse Foundation, the Leelanau County Road Commission, the *Grand Rapids Press*, Curt Teich Postcard Archives, and Avery Color Studios.

For use of their historical promotional materials we thank Hal Van Sumeren of the Traverse City Area Chamber of Commerce and Linda Singer of the West Michigan Tourist Association.

For use of photos in their archives we thank Susan Nichols of Fountain Point Resort, JoAnn Benjamin of the Homestead, and Ralph and Rose Gladfelter of the Sylvan Inn.

For making their private collections available to us we thank Jim Winslow, Ethel Paulina Furst Stomer, Marion Warnes, Steve Truman, George and Mollie Weeks, with special thanks to Jerry Conroy whose Leelanau County postcard collection is remarkable.

For use of his wonderful photos from the 1940s, 1950s, and 1960s, we would like to thank Phil Balyeat.

For her artistic hand-coloring of the historical photograph on the cover, our heartfelt thanks to Dianne Carroll-Burdick.

For their support and encouragement we thank Barbara Siepker of the Cottage Bookshop and Gordon Olson of the Grand Rapids Public Library.

For their advice, patience, perseverance, and technical assistance we thank Karolee Harris, Marcie Beck, and Dan Konkle.

Last, but certainly not least, special thanks to George and Mollie Weeks for their persistent encouragement, thoughtful suggestions, and helpful scholarship.

And for making it all happen, we thank Brian Lewis, our publisher.

To all those past and present, who have walked the beaches of Leelanau's shores, who have played in its blue-green waters, who have marveled at its sunsets, and who have slept under a blanket of Leelanau stars, this volume is dedicated.

M.C.B. and T.R.W.

Foreword

Few authors have captured the enchantment of "The Land of Delight" in words and images as vividly as Christine Byron and Tom Wilson have in this engaging book. Each page offers a masterful matching of vintage views and contemporaneous comments from newspaper articles and ads, or travel brochures, or, most delightfully, from postcards sent to family and friends by visitors themselves. It is a travel guide through Leelanau County's past from the travelers' perspective.

"Enjoying our stay here very much," said a "Dear Folks" postcard sent to Grand Rapids by "Delia" from Empire Aug. 16, 1930. "Wonderful lake, good bathing and fishing. Scenery grand." From the Glen Haven State Park, "Floyd" wrote to Freeland, Mich., July 28, 1927: "This is a beautiful country. Glen Lake looks like some of the pictures of the lakes in Ireland."

Such links of past and present, and of images and words, are among the joys of *Vintage Views of Leelanau County*. The authors' use of postcards and early travel material (most from their own extensive collection) is impressive. So is their solid research and reflective writing on the county and its towns and villages.

The book is a marvelous mix of fun and facts. One fact-packed paragraph: "Progress touched Leelanau County in 1862 when the first State Road opened, connecting Northport with Traverse City. Telegraph lines went in about 1847, followed by telephone service in the 1900s. The first railroad came into Leelanau County in 1892 and by 1903 many villages had rail service."

Two aspects of progress touching Leelanau County are aptly described and illustrated by this book. One is the Great Lakes shipping and cruise lines so important in early settlement and later development of the entire Grand Traverse Region. Another was the promotion of good roads. The book pays well deserved tribute to D. H. Day of Glen Haven, whose leadership in promoting tourism and road-building in West Michigan was recognized in 2001 by the Michigan Legislature and Governor John Engler. M-109, a portion of which Day was instrumental in building, was given an official commemorative designation as "D. H. Day Highway."

Books such as this depend heavily on local and state archives for historical photographs and other material. Of particular importance here were the news and ads from local newspapers. Example: A 1904 ad in the *Leelanau Enterprise* notes the rates at the Hotel Hahenberg in Provemont (now Lake Leelanau) were "$1.00 per day. Specials by the week."

The *Enterprise*, in a 1944 commentary about Leelanau County's early pioneers from 18 or so countries, said they were so struck with the place that "most of them never left." The paper said that as a result of this infusion, "Leelanau has a history that is as unique as its natural beauty and geographical setting."

That history, including those who visited and later came back to stay, is reflected in the images and words superbly presented by Christine Byron and Tom Wilson.

— George Weeks
Detroit News columnist and Leelanau County author

Contents

Introduction 8

Leelanau — The "Land of Delight" 10

Transportation 22

Empire 38

Sleeping Bear Sand Dunes..46

Glen Haven...64

Glen Lake Region..82

Glen Arbor..112

Lake Leelanau Region 126

Leland..138

Northport & Northport Point 156

Omena 182

Suttons Bay 198

North & South Manitou Islands...206

Other Places 224

The Authors 237

Bibliography and Sources Cited..238

Credits 240

Introduction

With this book we are attempting to take the reader back to the time when Leelanau County began to be known as the "Land of Delight." We have used historical photographs, postcards, and advertisements to capture the spirit of the time. The words of earlier writers have portrayed the flavor of the time, some with flowery language that we find charming today. Messages from the backs of Leelanau County postcards invite us to share someone else's vacation, so long ago remembered. We have kept the various misspellings and inaccuracies from these historical writings and have presented them as originally written, matching those words with images from the same time period. Sometimes there was a wide time frame, but we tried to keep the images and words reasonably close. We used the term "circa" when an exact date was not known.

Our book is meant to present an overview of Leelanau's history, with a special emphasis on vacationing and tourism. It was not our intention to delve deep into the history of the early pioneer days and lumbering era. We tried to present the flavor of the past, without a scholarly attempt to document it. We realize that there are gaps and omissions in our coverage. In some instances, we simply could not find the images we were looking for, such as the Wisteria Hotel at Fouch, Camp Kohanna at Port Oneida and scenes of motorboating on Glen Lake or Lake Leelanau. The section on South Manitou Island could have used more photographs, but they are extremely rare and hard to find. We focused on the areas where tourism was an important factor in their development and did not try to include every village and settlement, nor the Fox Islands.

The book covers the time period from the 1890s to the 1960s. It was our decision to focus on the more distant past, and not to attempt to cover more recent history. Within this time range, thousands of Leelanau County postcards were produced. We have been postcard collectors for over 15 years and have

Reminiscences among the Birches, circa 1915

accumulated about 1,400 postcards from the county. We also have been collecting old Michigan travel booklets and brochures for many years. Most of the postcards in this book are from our collection. We have credited the sources of the postcards and photographs that are not from our collection.

We hope that you enjoy your time travel through the pages of our book. We certainly have enjoyed working on it. To paraphrase a saying, we hope that you COME TO LEELANAU where you will find happiness and beauty.

— *M. Christine Byron and Thomas R. Wilson*

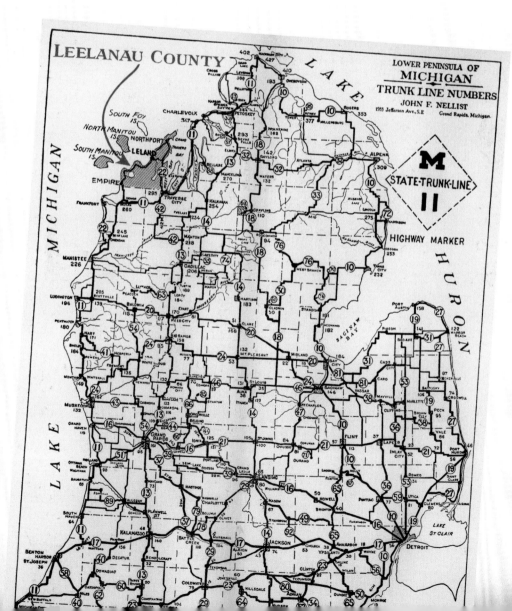

1947 MAP OF LEELANAU COUNTY
Traverse Bay Region, Michigan's Sunshine Corner
Traverse City Chamber of Commerce

MAP OF MICHIGAN, HIGHLIGHTING LEELANAU COUNTY
Leelanau County, The Land of Delight, 1926
Leelanau County is called the "little finger" of Michigan as it reaches out in Lake Michigan, which bounds it on three sides. Due to this surrounding water the climate is ideal, not too hot and not too cold. The pure refreshing breezes that come over the lake give the air a water-washed purity.

Leelanau – THE "LAND OF DELIGHT"

Leelanau County is bounded on the north and west by Lake Michigan, on the east by Grand Traverse Bay, and on the south by Benzie and Grand Traverse Counties. Its shape is an irregular triangle, with its greatest width being 22 miles, and its greatest length 29 miles. One hundred miles of shoreline define the peninsula, often called the "Little Finger" of the Michigan mitten.

For a long time it was believed that "Leelanau" was a Native American word that meant "land of delight." There was also speculation that the name was of French derivation — the "lee" meaning protective shelter, and "eau" meaning water in French. "Leelanau" would thus be a land in the lee of the prevailing winds over the waters of Lake Michigan. However, this description does not fit so well, as much of Leelanau is not in the "lee."

It was probably Henry R. Schoolcraft who was responsible for the name. Schoolcraft was an Indian Agent for the U.S. government who was responsible for naming many of Michigan's counties, including Cheboygan, Kalkaska, Newago, and Manistee. Schoolcraft was a scholar as well as a woodsman, who made up names out of Greek and Latin to sound like Indian words. Schoolcraft said that "Leelanau" meant "delight of life," as told in his story, "Leelinau, or the Lost Daughter, an Odjibwa Tale." The story tells of an Indian maiden who lived along the south shore of Lake Superior. The tale is repeated in Longfellow's "The Song of Hiawatha." The name has survived with changed spellings. In any event, the legend of Leelanau's Native American origin has taken hold, for Leelanau County is truly a "land of delight."

The Native Americans of the Ottawa and Chippewa tribes were the first people to inhabit Leelanau County. According to Ottawa tradition, the oldest settlement was at Omena Point. A second band settled at Cathead Point at the tip of the peninsula. Other settlements were at Onumunese (Omumeneseville) and at Glen Arbor. The largest Native American village, near Leland, was called "Che-ma-go-ming" or "Mishi-mi-go-bing."

The very nature of a peninsula assured that the first settlers would arrive by water. Almost all the vessel traffic plying Lake Michigan and the Straits of Mackinac traveled through the Manitou Passage. The six-mile passage separated South Manitou Island from Sleeping Bear Point on the mainland. Because of its strategic location and dangerous waters, the U.S. government established a lighthouse on South Manitou in 1839 to guide ships through the passage. A second lighthouse was built on North Manitou Island in 1898. To aid ships in distress and help victims of shipwrecks, three U. S. Life-Saving

Service stations were established along the Manitou Passage. The first was established on North Manitou Island in 1854. Sleeping Bear Point followed in 1901 and South Manitou Island in 1902.

The first European settler in what is now Leelanau County was William Burton (Barton), who established a wooding station on South Manitou Island in 1838. At the time of his settlement, South Manitou was part of Manitou County, as were North Manitou, the Fox Islands, and the Beaver Islands. For many early settlers the Manitou Islands served as a "stepping-stone" before they reached their final destination on the mainland. It was from South Manitou Island that in 1848 John La Rue moved to the mainland to settle in Glen Arbor, thus becoming the first European settler on Leelanau's mainland.

The mainland portion of Leelanau County was originally a township attached to Grand Traverse County. Leelanau became a separate county in 1863 with three large townships: Centerville, Glen Arbor, and Leelanau. That same year the county was reorganized, adding two new townships, Bingham and Elmwood. Six additional townships were created between 1865 and 1885: Kasson, Empire, Cleveland, Solon, Leland, and Suttons Bay, bringing the total to the current 11 townships. When Manitou County was dissolved in 1895, the Manitou and Fox Islands became part of Leelanau County. The first county seat was established in Northport in 1863, but moved to Leland in 1883.

In the early days of Leelanau County, almost all the land was covered with timber. The first commerce was supplying cordwood to the passing ships. These wooding stations were established at various locations along Leelanau County's shore. Soon logging operations expanded into the interior and sawmills were built to cut the newly harvested timber. The milled wood was shipped to Chicago and other Great Lakes ports. Lumbering reached its peak in Leelanau County about 1895-1900.

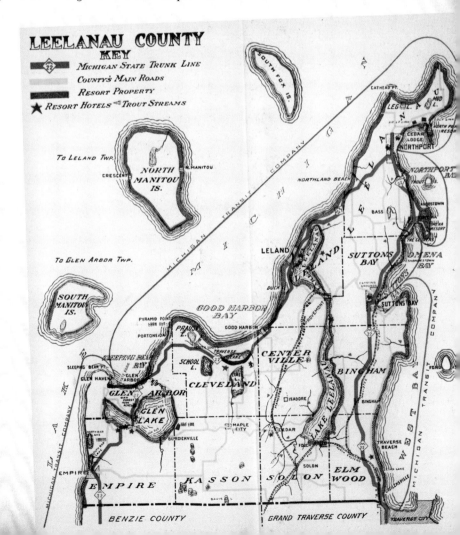

MAP OF LEELANAU COUNTY
Leelanau County, The Land of Delight, 1926

It seems to us, as we gazed upon the beautiful scenery that met our eyes at every turn, that we found the "Eldorado." The forests were unbroken; the axe of the white man had not marred its beauty; the beach of the bay was not strewn with refuse of the sawmill, but all lay in the state that Dame Nature had kept it, beautiful beyond description.

—James J. McLaughlin, 1849 as quoted in Power's *History of Northern Michigan*, 1912

The cutover lands were purchased by farmers who cleared the stumps to open the land for farming. At first, potatoes were the primary crop. Then in the 1850s the first cherry trees were planted and fruit farming eventually developed into a major activity.

Progress touched Leelanau County in 1862 when the first State Road opened, connecting Northport with Traverse City. Telegraph lines went in about 1874, followed by telephone service in the 1900s. The first railroad came into Leelanau County in 1892 and by 1903 many villages had rail service. Meanwhile churches, schools, and businesses supported an active community life in the growing villages.

By the 1890s Leelanau County was gaining a reputation for its fine summer resorts. Omena was home to the earliest resorts including the Leelanau Hotel, the Omena Inn, the Clovers, and the Sunset Lodge. Fountain Point on Lake Leelanau opened its doors to summer guests in 1889. At Northport Point, the Cedar Lodge opened in 1900. By 1911 Glen Lake had six resorts along its shore. Glen Haven, Glen Arbor, Empire, Leland, and Suttons Bay all had early hotels that were converted to the tourist trade.

The growth of the tourist trade in Leelanau County was partly due to the promotional materials that were published extolling Leelanau's virtues as a summer paradise. *Beauty Spots in Leelanau, 1901 Souvenir* applauded the Alpine scenery, the beautiful sunsets, the pure water of the lakes and streams, and the cool and bracing air which offered relief from the heat of the sweltering cities. The very atmosphere was said to have a beneficial effect on people suffering from malaria or hay fever. Other promotional materials followed and soon more and more summer vacationers were lured to Leelanau County. Bathing, boating, fishing, hunting, tennis, and golf were some of the amusements offered to the vacationer.

As automobile touring became more popular, Leelanau County's scenic drives were promoted. Lookouts, turnouts, and viewing towers presented the full splendor of the region to motorists. M-22 offered motorists views of Lake Michigan, Lake Leelanau, Glen Lake, and Traverse Lake as well as panoramas of cherry orchards, rolling hills, and woodlands. Travel writers "discovered" Leelanau County and featured such tourist attractions as Sleeping Bear Sand Dunes and its famous "dunes-mobile" rides, Glen Lake, and Leland's Fishtown, and more visitors came to the area.

To accommodate these visitors, cottage and cabin camps sprang up all over the county in the 1930s, 1940s, and 1950s. Camping facilities were offered at some parks, including D.H. Day State Park in Glen Haven. Northport and Suttons Bay established tourist camps, and Glen Lake and Lime Lake opened trailer parks.

Summer camps drew many young visitors to Leelanau County. Camp Leelanau for Boys, near Glen Arbor, was started in 1921 by William Beals, and Camp Kohanna for Girls, near Port Oneida, was established a few years later. Camp Caho, a girls' camp at Northport, opened in 1916 and Shady Trails, a speech improvement camp for boys, started operations in 1932.

Even with gas rationing and price controls on ice-cream cones, Leelanau continued to attract vacationers during World War II. Newspaper articles noted that it was located well out of the defense area, and that one needed a vacation to be able to perform one's job more productively. Middle class family vacations became commonplace in the 1950s and hundreds of families spent a week or two in Leelanau County each year. Today many of those baby boomers have happy memories of the "Land of Delight" and have returned to vacation with their own families or to build summer homes.

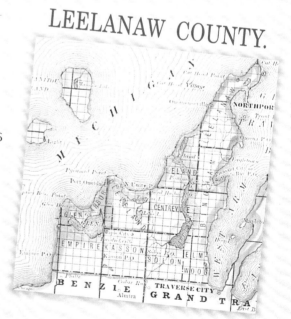

LEELANAW COUNTY.

1884 MAP OF LEELANAU COUNTY

In the early days, when Leelanau was a new word in Michigan history, someone at Lansing, in copying this name made a mistake changing the final u to w. So for a time, two ways of spelling it prevailed; but in 1897 it was officially recognized as L-e-e-l-a-n-a-u, and that year the Michigan Gazeteer, and all other official documents used the correct spelling.

— *Leelanau Enterprise*, July 16, 1936

"Vacation Handbook and Fisherman's Guide, Leelanau County"

— *Leelanau Enterprise*, 1939

The peninsula of Leelanau has been the scene of many important events that have taken place in the Grand Traverse region during the last 100 years. Most of the early settlers that came to the Grand Traverse region, first landed on either North or South Manitou Islands, later to come across to the main land. This was a natural procedure, since the excellent semicircular harbor of South Manitou Island was the best ship refuge between Chicago and the Straits of Mackinac. Almost all ship traffic plying between the ports of southern Lake Michigan and the Mackinac Straits, utilized the Manitou Passage, and with both North Manitou and South Manitou Islands serving as the main wooding stations between the northern and southern ends of the lake, just about every steam boat stopped at one or the other island for fuel. And so by virtue of the Manitou Passage, the peninsula of Leelanau has played an important role in the early history of northern Michigan and the Grand Traverse region in particular. Almost every well known family name in the region today found its way here through the original immigrant stock that landed on one of the Manitou Islands and later coming to the Leelanau mainland or whatever other part of the region might be chosen for a permanent home.

A good part of the pioneer population came to the region by the overland route through the southern part of the state, during the 1850s and 1860s. Most of them used a team of oxen to haul their worldly belongings. The roads from the south, leading to Leelanau were only trails that were just wide enough for wagons to pass. This method of travel was slow and tedious, and often days were required to cover a few hundred miles. They went through hardships few of us can visualize. There are a few of the county's early pioneers still living that arrived either by the overland route or by the water route, stopping first at the islands. About eighteen different countries were represented in the early pioneer population of the county.

The beauty of the Leelanau peninsula was the stimulus that formed their first impression of the region, and most of them never left.

For these reasons, Leelanau has a history that is as unique as its natural beauty and geographical setting.

— *Leelanau Enterprise*, December 14, 1944

Logging Scene

In the early days of Leelanau County's history almost all of the land was covered with hardwood, with some softwood patches of pine, hemlock, and cedar. The lumberjacks first used axes to fell the trees, but later saws were used. Much of the cut timber was sold as cordwood to the steamers traveling through the Manitou Passage. Winter provided the loggers an easy way to transport their harvest. Logs were placed on a sleigh and pulled by a team of horses or oxen. Sawmills cut the logs into lumber for shipment to Chicago and other ports. Lumbering reached its peak in Leelanau County about 1895 — 1900. As the lumbering industry waned, tourism began to develop.

Romance of the inland seas is written big in the annals of the Glen Lake district, one of the concentration points for shipping on Lake Michigan.

Those on shore have watched the coming and goings of ships for years and years. They have seen their lights plowing through the summer seas, slipping silently along during the night, and have witnessed the death struggles in the winter surf as the big lake monarchs have battled vainly to keep off shore when the wintry gales are washing them toward shore and destruction.

The government, that good father of all shipping, has recognized the uncertainty of the inland seas and has come to the aid of the sailors who spend their lives on ships. Life saving stations have been established at Sleeping Bear Point and another on North Manitou Island and the light houses blink forth their way rays nightly from the two Manitous, watching the lights off shore, say silent little prayers that the ships may keep off the dangerous shores.

— *Traverse City Record Eagle,* July 31, 1926

Life Saving Station, North Manitou

Song of Leelanau

Words by the late Charles Howard Thomas

1. Thou are a grand pen-in-su-la,
   "Land of De-light"—Thou Leelanau.
   Great in-land seas thy borders lave,
   Thy moun-tains tower a-bove the wave.

   CHORUS
   Grand Lee-la-nau! "Land of De-light!"
   from Sugar Loaf behold the sight!
   Of wooded hills and valleys green,
   Where fountains flow with living stream.
   The Sleeping Bear, and Manitou,
   "Land of De-light"—Thou Leelanau.

2. Thy lakes reflecting Heaven's blue,
   Thy thou-sand scenes of matchless view,
   Thy winding roads mid for-ests rare,
   Be-speak God's bles-sing ev'ry-where.

3. Thy ap-ple or-chards droop-ing deep,
   With lucious load and painted cheek,
   Thy cher-ries bloom at Spring's sweet call,
   And fruit-ing yield the best of all.

4. Great ships de-light thy ports to make;
   The rich, the poor, thy bounties take;
   Thy fruit-ful lands rare pro-ducts grow;
   A par-a-dise, Thou Leelanau.

5. Thy wealth of scene and health-ful air,
   Give rest for toil and joy for care,
   And pil-grims come from every clime,
   To find in thee the land sublime.

6. For thee blest land of joy and health,
   Endowed with God's most gracious wealth.
   We bow the head in rev-'rent awe,
   And thanks we give for Leelanau.

— "Vacation Handbook and Fisherman's Guide, Leelanau County,"
Leelanau Enterprise, 1939

Swiss Inn Launch Party

We (Leelanau County) have Alpine scenery, Italian sunsets, and woodland perfumes equal to the most fragrant exotics of the Orient. The water of our lakes and streams and bays is pure, sparkling, cold, the nectar of the gods. It is found everywhere trickling from the hillsides, bubbling up by the road-side, ever the same pure life-giving liquid that reaches the thirst of the feverish invalid and cools the heated brow of the college athletic. The air, cool and bracing. To the tired, overworked business man, shut up in a stuffy dark office, bound in by brick walls, heated by the combined forces of nature and over strung nerves, it is a rejuvenator, a renovator, and exhilarator to draw in a full breath of it. It is the real elixir of life. It makes the blood jump and tingle and you are new again.

— *Beauty Spots in Leelanau, 1901 Souvenir*

Leelanau—'Land of Delight,' the Indians named it!

Bathing in Crystal River at Glen Arbor Mich.

And how could the name have been more appropriate? Washed on three sides by the cold rollers of great expanses of water, it is no wonder that the Leelanau peninsula is the coolest region in the summer months of the year. It is as if a Divine Being had fashioned by its own hand an ideal and perfect spot for humanity to play and enjoy itself in its vacation time.

Everything seems to have been planned with the same ideal of perfection. As far as the eye can reach, gaze falls upon timber-covered hills, sheltered harbors, mystic hazy islands, overhanging rugged bluffs, hidden unexplored lakes, long stretches of pure white sandy beaches fading away in the distance.

Behind all this peaceful natural beauty hides tradition, the very soul of the land—tales of Indians, forgotten tribes, deeds of horror and deeds of bravery, stories of romance and adventure. The past existence of these ancient dwellers of the land seems to permeate the very air we breathe.

And yet, through all this quiet atmosphere, we seem to sense something different and foreign—a feeling of progress, improvement, and building. Yes, through all that land of Nature, a new movement is coming and has come. In scattered spots, Nature has been improved upon. Undergrowth and scraggly trees have been cleared away to make room for dwelling houses, towns, industries, rolling plains covered with rich cherry orchards.

What a new note it all strikes in us this fast-developing civilization thrown into sharp contrast with Mother Nature, unimproved and unshorn of her original beauties. But here it all is, and preserved unchanged.

Ten years ago, one would have had to give up many of your comforts to be a witness to the vast spectacle, but now pleasant little resort centers, established in various scattered places over Leelanau County are waiting to fulfill your every need. You owe yourself a rest.

Why not journey to this vacation land of all lands and really enjoy yourself this summer?

— *Traverse City Record Eagle,* June 30, 1933

Leelanau Peninsula—
what shall we call it?

Dunesland.
Cherryland. Lakeland.
Fishingland. Cedarland. Hillyland.
Resortland. Bayland. Legendland. Viewland.
Any one of these describes it. And all of them fit.

...The peninsula might be called Dunesland because of the massive, creeping Sleeping Bear sand dunes along its southwestern edge. It might be called Cherryland because of the fruitful orchards of nation-wide fame that thrive in its water-tempered, water-washed air. It might be called Lakeland because of its total area of 216,320 acres embraces beautiful Glen Lake, 7,680 acres, elongated Lake Leelanau, 8,960 acres, and a score of smaller lakes. The fishing in these lakes, as well as in Grand Traverse Bay and Lake Michigan, and the commercial fishing hamlets along the shore of the peninsula give it the right to be known as Fishingland.

Millions of cedars lend their beauty to the peninsula and hence the designation Cedarland. High hills along the base of the peninsula and up through the center providing mountainous scenery give it a right to be known as Hillyland.

Long before the coming of the automobile and the building of Highway M-22 — which encircles the peninsula — this region was popular with summer visitors. Good roads and easy access have increased the number of tourists and cottagers so Leelanau is outstandingly a Resortland.

Bays along its shore — Sleeping Bear and Good Harbor on the Lake Michigan side; Northport, Sutton's and Omena on the Grand Traverse side — as well as 37 miles of shoreline on the Grand Traverse Bay, make Bayland appropriate.

Indians still dwell on Leelanau Peninsula, and the region is rich in traditions of the long ago. There are tales of the red men who sought to invade the region from the west; there are tales of animal adventuring, such as caused the great Manitou to turn a mother bear into Sleeping Bear Dune, and her cubs into the two Manitou Islands, just off the coast of the peninsula. Hence the area may be called Legendland.

And anyone who has traveled the peninsula knows why the term Viewland is particularly pertinent. The landscapes and marinescapes from the heights around Glen Lake and from the hills overlooking Grand Traverse Bay are breathtaking in their beauty. Wherever one goes along M-22, on the county roads, or on hikes, there are nature pictures of rare interest.

— Stace, *Michigan's Tourist Attractions*, 1940

Where to Fish!

*Leelanau County abounds in Inland Lakes and Streams
of Sparkling, Clear Water, Affording Fine Fishing Advantages*

GLEN LAKE — *Trout, Bass, Pike, Perch, Blue Gills*

LAKE LEELANAU — *Muskellunge, Trout, Bass, Pike, Perch, Blue Gills, Sun Fish*

TRAVERSE LAKE — *Bass, Pike, Perch, Blue Gills*

LIME LAKE — *Bass, Pike, Perch*

CEDAR RUN — *Trout Fishing*

LAKE MICHIGAN — *Trolling for Lake Trout*

AMONG THE BROOK TROUT STREAMS — *Houdek Creek, Cedar Run,
Shalda Creek, Belanger Creek*

— *Leelanau County, Michigan, The Land of Delight,* circa 1930

Keep Fit and Strong

*Arrangements are going to be made to permit vacation time for every
working man and woman. You need a vacation, to be able to carry on at
full capacity; you need relaxation and fun with which to re-energize, so
that you will go back to your work better able to work! Plan some vacation
period during the summer when you can be most easily spared...and come to
Leelanau County, where you will have a wonderful time.*

*Leelanau County, located well out of the defense area, is one of the
most beautiful counties in the state.*

*For the business man who would like to settle his family in this delightful
region without the use of their car, they will find our shopping facilities as convenient as home because the farmers call daily with fruits and garden truck.
Local food and general merchandise stores are located on most all lakes or
nearby, making it easy for the family to shop.*

*As this county is surrounded by water, it makes an ideal place for the
hayfever sufferers.*

— *Traverse City Record Eagle,* June 30, 1942

Cherry Blossom Time at Suttons Bay

Leelanau's rolling hills are famous for the great cherry orchards which reach new heights of beauty at blossom time in the Spring.

— *Carefree Days in West Michigan*, West Michigan Tourist Association, 1940

Cherry Blossom Time at Suttons Bay, Mich.

Cherry Season at the Peak in Leelanau Now

With the sunny weather prevailing this week, conditions are ideal for the harvesting of the cherry crop. Sweet cherries have already been picked, but the bulk of the Montmorencies, or pie cherries, are being stripped from the trees this week.

Capacity of the canning factories is a big factor in determining the time of picking at the various orchards. The factories are being pushed to the limit, and it is sometimes necessary to ask orchard owners to stop picking for a day.

Leelanau's two factories, at Northport and Glen Haven, are handling much of the cherry crop of sour cherries, and many more are being shipped to Traverse City to the canneries there.

A vast army of pickers has employment for a couple of weeks, and yet there is a surplus of laborers. Many people have come in from outside in search of work in the orchards…

A prospective price of 3¢ per pound is giving the growers a better outlook than in the last two years. The prevailing price for picking is about a ½¢ per pound, which leaves 2½¢ for hauling, spraying, cultivation and other expenses.

— Leelanau Enterprise, July 27, 1933

Transportation

Unlike many parts of the country that were settled by pioneers traveling overland, Leelanau County was settled by people who arrived by ship. Early transportation to Leelanau was by water, first by sailing vessels then by steamers. The first settlements were located near the county's natural harbors — South Manitou, Glen Arbor, Northport, Omena, Leland, Suttons Bay, and Glen Haven.

In the early nineteenth century steam side-wheelers began to ply the waters of the western Great Lakes and settlements arose to supply the cordwood that was their fuel. Around 1840 a wooding station was established on South Manitou Island and within a few years another on North Manitou, and soon others at Glen Arbor, Glen Haven, and Leland. There were four wooding stations at Northport, which because of its large safe harbor and plentiful wood supply was a popular stop for the 400 steamers that were sailing the Great Lakes by the mid 1850s.

As the nineteenth century wore on, the side-wheel steamers began to be replaced by the faster and more seaworthy propeller driven steamers, often called "propellers" to distinguish them from side-wheelers. These propellers operated out of many ports-of-call on the Great Lakes, including Detroit, Cleveland, and Buffalo and provided transportation to settlers coming into the area and later for tourists visiting the region.

In 1893 there were two main steamship lines competing in Northern Michigan, the Seymour line out of Manistee and the Northern Michigan Transportation Company out of Chicago. By 1895 the two lines had merged and kept the name of the Northern Michigan Transportation Company. In 1918 the name was changed to the Michigan Transit Company. The MTC operated the larger ships serving the area with connections to Chicago and eastern ports such as Detroit, Cleveland, Buffalo, and Montreal. The steamers *Illinois*, *Missouri*, *Manitou*, and *Puritan* were operated by the MTC. These ships served the heavily traveled Chicago to Mackinac route, making stops in Leelanau County at Glen Haven, Glen Arbor, Leland, and Northport, bringing thousands of vacationers to Leelanau County each summer.

In addition to the major steamships there were also smaller steamers that provided service along Grand Traverse Bay from Traverse City to Suttons Bay, Omena, Northport, Charlevoix, and Petoskey. The Traverse Bay Line of steamers operated from 1887 to 1906 with three steamers—the *Crescent*, *Columbia*, and *Lou A. Cummings*. The steamer line lost many of its passengers when rail service took hold and consequently ceased its operations in 1906. Despite that failure, a new company was formed,

Traverse Bay Transportation, which operated the steamer *Chequamegon* until 1911. The *Chequamegon* ran from Traverse City to Charlevoix, stopping at Basset Island, Neahtawanta, Omena, and Northport.

At the dawn of the twentieth century shipping and travel on the Great Lakes were at their peak, and it was not unusual for 50 or more ships a day to sail through the Manitou Passage. The passage was only six miles wide with rocky shoals, and the weather could be unpredictable, all of which made for dangerous travel. Lighthouses were built to guide ships and lifesaving stations were established to aid ships in distress.

Meanwhile, as the settlement of Leelanau continued in the mid-1800s and the need for travel between the settlements grew, an increased need for travel overland led to the development of state roads. The first roads were crude paths that led from one settlement to the next and did not provide for continuous travel over any great distance. These roads were used for horse-and-buggies and wagons. It was not until the 1860s that much progress was made in the construction of continuous state roads in the region. The first state road opened in 1862, called the Northport to Newaygo Road, and ran in Leelanau County from Traverse City to Northport, following an old Native American trail.

After the Civil War, stagecoach service was established between villages, with most having service two or three times a week. The stage provided means of both travel and communication to such important places as Northport (the county seat until 1883), and Traverse City, the nearest banking point. The stagecoach lines carried the mail until the railroads were established. They also provided service to port cities that had access to steamships, which were the still major mode of transportation.

The first railroad came to Leelanau County in 1892 when the Manistee and Northeastern Railroad completed the route from Manistee to Traverse City. Two stops were established in Leelanau County — one at Solon and another at Fouch. A branch line was added to Cedar a few years later. Rail service to Fouch allowed travelers to make connections with the steamers that ran the length of Lake Leelanau and made possible a day trip from Leland to Traverse City.

STEAMSHIP *Manitou*

Additional railroad activity began in 1900 as two rail lines competed to reach Northport. The Manistee and Northeastern pushed on to Provemont (Lake Leelanau) in 1903, but never extended its line beyond the narrows of Lake Leelanau. At the same time the Traverse City, Leelanau and Manistique Railroad completed its line all the way to Northport, with stops at Greilickville, Hatch's Crossing, Bingham, Keswick, Suttons Bay, and Omena. The T.C.L. & M. had the encouragement, if not the outright backing of the Grand Rapids and Indiana Railroad, which wanted to see ferry service provided from Northport to Manistique to enable its trains to connect with lines in the Upper Peninsula.

In June of 1903 the T.C.L. & M. began service to Omena, Suttons Bay, and Northport with the ferry service beginning in October of the same year. Freight traffic between Northport and Manistique never developed to a profitable level and the ferry service was discontinued in 1908. The T.C.L. & M. continued to operate rail service between Traverse City and Northport. The line changed hands after WW I and was operated by the Manistee and Northeastern, then later by the Pere Marquette before being abandoned in the 1970s.

About the same time that rail service to Northport was established, the first automobiles began to appear in Leelanau County. These early autos were very expensive and only the wealthy could afford them. In 1904 even an inexpensive auto such as an Oldsmobile or a Ford cost $850, an enormous sum for the average family. It took Henry Ford producing cars in large quantities to drive the price down to $345. Then as more people bought cars, the need for improved roads increased.

The earliest and most ardent promoter of better roads in Leelanau County was D.H. Day. From its inception in 1911, Day was involved in the West Michigan Pike Association, which worked to build one continuous road from Michigan City to Mackinaw City. He was also instrumental in the promotion of M-22 as a scenic loop to the West Michigan Pike (later U.S. 31) in an effort to encourage tourism in the county.

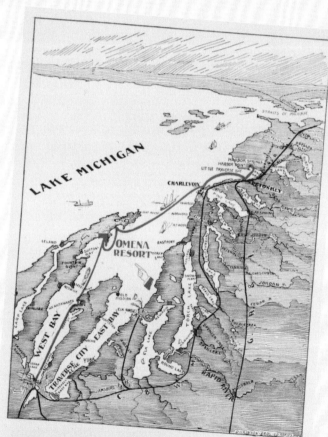

ADVERTISEMENT — TRAVERSE BAY LINE OF STEAMERS
— *Omena Resort*, circa 1901

"Good roads" in the 1920s generally meant good *gravel* roads. Only a few villages had paved streets. M-22 in Glen Arbor was paved with cement in 1925 and a section in Leland was paved in 1928. Other portions of M-22 were paved gradually. The last section between Suttons Bay and Northport was completed in 1954.

From the beginning of the twentieth century, touring the scenic roads of Leelanau County was enjoyed by many travelers, first by horse-and-buggy and later by automobile. The many lookouts and scenic vistas showcased Leelanau's rolling hills, cherry orchards, woodlands, lakes, and rivers. M-22 has been cited as one of the most beautiful drives in the country and has been designated a Michigan Scenic Heritage Route.

The automobile changed the way Americans traveled. Motoring offered an ease of mobility and freedom to wander the countryside. For these reasons automobile travel supplanted steamship and rail travel. Whatever means of transportation that people used over the years, it was the scenic beauty that lured them to Leelanau County.

The Traverse Bay Line of steamers are the Columbia, Crescent, *and* Cummings, *owned by H.J. Webb of Cassopolis. These boats run out of Traverse City and Petoskey, making all points along the shore. The* Crescent *leaves Traverse City every day at 2:00 p.m. for Northport and Northport Point Resort, stopping at Neahtawanta, Suttons Bay, and Omena; returning she leaves Northport at 7:00 p.m., arriving at Traverse City in time to connect with trains for the South. A boat also leaves Traverse City every morning over this route, returning the same day, making a delightful trip.*

The service usually is put on about June 15th. Another of this line plies between Northport and Northport Point and Norwood, Charlevoix, Petoskey, and connecting at Harbor Springs with the Great Lakes steamships, Northland, Northwest, *and* Manitou, *which run this season between Chicago and Buffalo. For rates and particulars, address H.J. Webb, Traverse City, Mich.*

These boats have been put in excellent condition for this season's trade, and will be found clean, neat and comfortable. The boatmen will be found obliging, courteous gentlemen who have the interest of their passengers always at heart. Write H.J. Webb, Traverse City, Mich., for time card for season of 1901.

— Beauty Spots in Leelanau, 1901 Souvenir

Columbia – Traverse Bay Line

Northern Michigan Transportation Company, 1911

The Northern Michigan Transportation Company served Northern Michigan ports from Ludington to Mackinac Island. They operated the steamships *Puritan*, *Manitou*, *Illinois*, and *Missouri*. The ships were luxurious for their time. The *S.S. Manitou* had "commodious" staterooms and parlors, berths of ample size, and complete furnishings. Everything was provided to make the traveler comfortable and social gatherings enjoyable, including spacious decks and inviting easy chairs. Its Leelanau County ports of call included Glen Haven, Glen Arbor, Northport, and Suttons Bay.

Afternoon Train Approaching Northport, circa 1910

The train from Traverse City to Northport ran daily and took two hours, stopping at several small stations along the way.

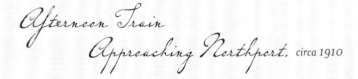

Traverse City, Leelanau & Manistique R. R.

Operated by UNION TRUST, CO., Receiver.

Time Table No. 1. Taking Effect at 6 A. M., Dec. 30, 1906.

NORTHWARD TRAINS.				SOUTHWARD TRAINS.
FIRST CLASS				FIRST CLASS
91	Distance			90
DAILY EXCEPT SUNDAY		STATIONS.		DAILY EXCEPT SUNDAY
P. M. 3.40		TRAVERSE CITY ... D		A. M. 10.05
		1.77		
s 4.05	5.7	HATCH'S CROSSING ... D		s 9.45
		1.95		
f 4.10	7.7	HEINFORTH		f 9.40
		1.99		
s 4.16	9.6	BINGHAM		s 9.30
		1.87		
f 4.21	11.5	KESWICK		f 9.20
		1.84		
f 4.26	13.3	LEELANAU		f 9.10
		3.38		
s 4.50	16.7	SUTTON'S BAY ... D		s 8.50
		7.00		
s 5.10	23.7	OMENA		s 8.20
		0.50		
5.12	24.2	"OA" SIDING		8.15
		4.75		
s 5.30	29.2	NORTHPORT ... D		s 8.00
P. M.				A. M.

STANDARD CLOCK–Traverse City Telegraph office.
BULLETIN BOOKS Traverse City Telegraph office.
REGISTERING STATIONS Traverse City M. & N. E. Telegraph office. Traverse City M. & N. E. Telegraph office. Hatch's Crossing Telegraph office. Northport Telegraph office.
YARD LIMIT BOARD–Northport.
Trains must not leave terminals without train orders or clearance.

Conductors and Enginemen using M. & N. E. tracks must provide themselves with M. & N. E. Time Table and be governed accordingly.
Southward trains are superior to Northward trains of the same class.
D—Day Telegraph office.
N—Night Telegraph office.
Employes will be governed by the rules of the G. R. & I. Ry. for the government of the Transportation Department.

J. H. P. HUGHART,
Agent for the Receiver.

J. W. HUNTER

Manistique and Northern Ferry No. 1

The *Manistique, Marquette and Northern Ferry No. 1* operated between Northport and Manistique from 1903 to 1908. At 338 feet it was one of the longest ferries on the Great Lakes. The 75 mile crossing took 11 hours.

Manistique Marquette and Northern Ferry № 1 at Northport, Mich.

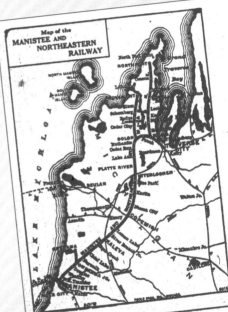

MANISTEE & NORTH-EASTERN R.R.

THE MICHIGAN TRUST COMPANY, Receiver

NOT GOOD FOR PASSAGE

Conductors will preserve this half of Duplex Tickets used, and after making up their report from them at end of trip return them to Auditor with their Ticket collections.

A. N. HEUSS, Gen'l Passenger Agent

No. 9827½

Through the Heart of the Vacation Land

that's the route of the

MANISTEE & NORTHEASTERN RAILWAY

Established 1887.

Leelanau County Schedule

Train No. 6—For Cedar and Provement—Leaves Traverse City at 6:15 a. m.
Train No. 7—From Cedar and Provement—Arrives in Traverse City at 9:00 a. m.
Train No. 8—For Suttons Bay and Northport—Leaves Traverse City at 3:00 p. m. (Except Saturday—at 2:00 p. m.)
Train No. 9—From Suttons Bay and Northport—Arrives in Traverse City at 6:22 p. m.
(Except Saturday—at 5:22 p. m.)

Traverse City and Manistee Schedule

Train for Manistee leaves Traverse City at 9:45 a. m., over P. M. R. R. (From Pere Marquette Station), Arrives at Kaleva at 10:48 a. m. Leaves Kaleva over M. & N. E. at 11:00 a. m. Arrives at Manistee at 11:45 a. m.
Train for Traverse City leaves Manistee at 9:50 a. m. over M. & N. E. for Kaleva. Arrives in Kaleva at 10:30 a. m. Leaves Kaleva over P. M. R. R. at 10:48 a. m. Arrives in Traverse City at 11:55 a. m.

(The Time Shown on Above Schedule is Central Standard Time)

GENERAL OFFICES: MANISTEE, MICH.

J. GORDON JOHNSON, General Manager and Traffic Manager.

After struggling for several years, the Traverse City, Leelanau and Manistique Railroad became part of the Manistee and Northeastern Railroad in 1919.

ADVERTISEMENT — MANISTEE AND NORTHEASTERN R.R.
— *Traverse City Record Eagle*, 1933

The Depot, Northport

The Northport Depot was built about 1920 in the mirror image of
the Suttons Bay depot. The fieldstone building saw rail service
under the Manistee and Northeastern Railroad, the Pere
Marquette Railroad, and later the Chesapeake and Ohio Railroad.

Horse-and-buggy,
Sunday Drive

These early vacationers stopped to pose for the camera while out for a Sunday buggy ride along the shores of Glen Lake. Scenic drives lured visitors to explore the natural beauty of the Glen Lake area. Circa 1900.

Along Glen Lake

The county roads in Leelanau County are probably as good for driving or bicycling as are found in any primitive facilities. There are hills and sand and all that make country roads, but most of them are graveled and smooth, and there are miles of road that wind in and out among the densest shade through sylvan dells leading out to some of the most picturesque scenery in the world. There are high hills, almost mountains — lakes, ravines, water falls, and the densest growth of evergreens and deciduous trees that you would wish to tread in your search for beauty spots.

— *Beauty Spot in Leelanau, 1901 Souvenir*

Along Glen Lake

First Car in Leelanau County

The first car in Leelanau County was nicknamed the "Red Devil" and owned by Dr. Fralick of Maple City. Motoring was an adventure on the early roads of Leelanau County, which were not much more than dirt paths. The motorist did not know what to expect. Washouts, mud holes, livestock, badly marked detours, could loom around the next bend in the road.

Tobin's Store,
Glen Lake

Tobin's Store, Glen Lake, Mich.

Before numbered roads with signage, the motorist would depend upon directions such as these to find his destination

Empire to Glen Arbor, Michigan

6.9 miles

.0 Leave 3-corners at general store, go east on gravel road to 4-corners, school house on near right

.2 Turn left (road straight ahead goes to Traverse City)

.3 Pass road on left to 3-corners

.4 Turn right, cross R.R.

.6 Benzie-Leelanau Fair Grounds on right, shortly go up grade, continue on gravel road

2.2 Pass on left (which goes to Glen Haven via Michigan Pike)

3.0 Curve left with road to four corners

4.2 Turn right to irregular 4-corners at Tobin's grocery on left

5.0 Turn left along Glen Lake on left, cross levee and bridge over neck of Glen Lake

5.5 Curve right along Glen Lake on right through woods, continue to end of road, store on near right

6.8 Turn right (Note: Road on left goes to Sylvan Inn — 1 block where fine meal and sleeping accommodations may be had).

6.9 Glen Arbor

— *King's Official Route Guide,* 1920

Opposite page: D.H. Day Putting Up Road Signs

This photograph shows D.H. Day, on the far right, placing the first West Michigan Pike sign in Leelanau County. The West Michigan Pike followed the "lakeshore all the way" along Michigan's western coast from Michigan City to Mackinaw City. As the Leelanau County director of the West Michigan Pike Association, Day staged auto rallies in Glen Haven as part of the annual West Michigan Pike tours.

Indication of Big Resort Season

One of the best tests for knowing the amount of summer business being done in a certain region and the number of summer people visiting that region is to observe the amount of express and baggage arriving over the railroads. While most of the resorters come now by car, yet the bulk of their baggage and express comes by rail.

P.A. Shettik, the genial station agent, says that incoming baggage and express this year already amounts to more than for the last two seasons combined. This of course, can mean nothing else than that Leelanau County is entertaining more summer people than ever before. It means that more people are learning the delights of our county and are availing themselves of the opportunity of coming here.

Another indication of the continued growth of this business is an unusually large sale of building material. Many new cottages are under construction and others are undergoing extensive improvements.

— Leelanau Enterprise, July 14, 1927

Leelanau Roads a Lure for Tourists

You will enjoy driving the roads in Leelanau County. From numerous mountain views along the highways one can see the wooded hills, beautiful farm lands against the setting of many pretty lakes of the county, and at the same time it will take you thru our beautiful resort areas which are always about you. There is a new drive for every day of the week, and many of the drives and lookout spots you will want to visit many times, they are so fascinating.

The road system of Leelanau County comprises 677 miles, 104 miles of this system is hard surfaced, 303 miles improved with gravel surfacing, and 270 miles unimproved but in good shape for traveling. The County Road Commission has long been noted for its efficiency in building and maintaining the roads of the county.

— *Traverse City Record Eagle*, July 28, 1938

*Glen Lake Drive,
Leelanau County, Michigan*

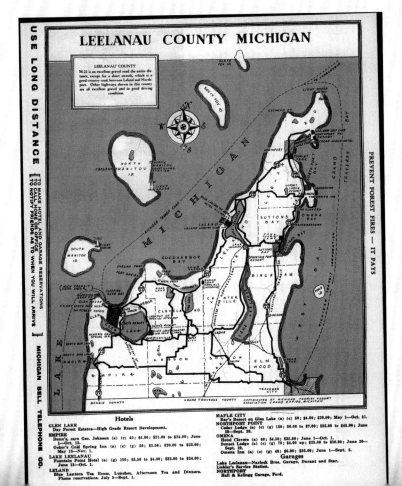

Map of Leelanau County, *West Michigan Vacation Directory*, 1929
This 1929 map follows the scenic M-22 "around the horn." The upper left-hand insert refers to M-22 as an "excellent gravel road the entire distance, except for a short stretch, which is good country road, between Leland and Northport. Other highways shown in this county are all excellent gravel and in good driving condition." As a help to early motorists, hotels and garages were listed.

Suttons Bay, Peshawba Town, Omena, Northport,
Northport Point and return via Leland and Lake Leelanau

Round Trip, 75 miles

Leaving Traverse City on M-22 north, passing through farm and orchard region to Suttons
Bay. Through Suttons Bay north along bay shore to Peshawba Town, last stronghold of the
Indians in the Grand Traverse Region. Follow M-22 to Omena, one of the exclusive colonies
of Northern Michigan. Here a safe drive to Omena Point will take only a few minutes. From
Omena follow M-22 to Northport and out to Northport Point, where Cedar Lodge Hotel,
a cottage colony and golf course are located.

   "The Log Cabin" on the bluffs overlooking Lake Michigan makes a delightful side trip
of about three miles west of Northport.

   Returning, leave Northport on M-22, through Leland, a prominent summer resort, located at a point where Lake Leelanau
empties into Lake Michigan. It has several delightful summer hotels, cottages, golf courses, etc. On the left entering Leland is located
the Blue Lantern Tea Room. From Leland follow the shore of Lake Leelanau to the village of Lake Leelanau. Cross bridge over narrows.
To right lays beautiful Fountain Point Resort, with its ever-flowing fountain. Thence back on main highway southeast of village. Turn
south and follow road to shore of West Bay, then follow shore along scenic drive into Traverse City.

— Six Drives Out of Many Delightful Drives in the Immediate Vicinity of Traverse City, circa 1935

Anyone who comes into Northern Michigan and fails
to take the "grand tour" along M-22 in Leelanau
County has had only half a vacation. Every mile of
this 65-mile ride opens a new vista and every mile is
a pleasant thrill through Michigan's scenic county.

— Grand Traverse Bay Region: Michigan's
Sunshine Corner, 1947

The Grand Tour...*Even though not vacationing in Leelanau County, any person coming into the Grand Traverse Bay Region should not fail to take the Grand Tour around the horn. Leaving Traverse City on M-22 the motorist can follow the shore of Grand Traverse Bay, touching at Sutton's Bay, Peshawbestown, Omena, Northport, Leland, Glen Arbor, Glen Haven and Empire. This tour takes one around the entire perimeter of the county and along the water's edge seventy-five per cent of the way. In all of these small resort communities one may find excellent eating places and interesting shops.*

— *Vacation Days in the Grand Traverse Bay Region*, circa 1949

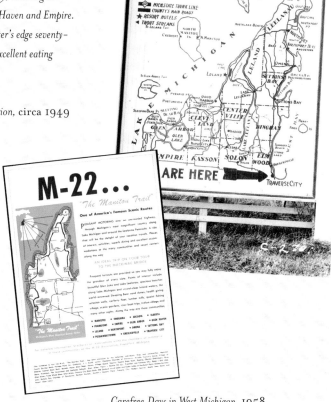

M-22...The Manitou Trail

In 1953 the M-22 Association had a contest to name route M-22 from Manistee to Traverse City. The winning entry was the "Manitou Trail," submitted by William H. Nash of Traverse City. His grand prize was $10.00.

Carefree Days in West Michigan, 1958

Overlooking Glen Lake, from Miller Hill

Roads to Happiness...Perhaps no other county offers more scenic drives than Leelanau. Up hill and down dale go the excellent highways which thread the county and from high hills may be seen beautiful lakes far below or glimpses of Lake Michigan with its ships passing. Long vistas of forested country unfold before the traveler as Leelanau's highways lead from one startling scene to another. Motoring in Leelanau is a very pleasant pastime.

— *Vacation Days in Michigan's Grand Traverse Bay Region*, 1961

Empire

Empire is located in the southwestern section of Leelanau county, 25 miles west of Traverse City and 27 miles southwest of Leland.

The first European settler was John La Rue. In 1864 La Rue moved south from Glen Arbor to settle in Empire near Otter Creek. He was followed by Pete Stormer in 1865 and then George Aylesworth in 1872. Aylesworth built a dock and cut and sold cordwood to the steamships that were bringing additional settlers to the area.

In 1885 Struthers & Potter built a lumber mill on the shore of Lake Michigan. The T. Wilce Company of Chicago formed the Empire Lumber Company and in 1887 purchased the Struthers & Potter mill and began to expand. E. Harvey Wilce, son of the founder, was named the manager of the Empire Lumber Company. The E.L.C. harvested timber, cut it into lumber and shipped the lumber to the T. Wilce factory in Chicago where it was made into tongue-and-groove flooring, in a process for which it held the patent.

In 1892 the E.L.C. began building a railroad to transport the cut timber. It became known as the Empire & South Eastern Railroad and connected with the Manistee and Northeastern Railroad at Empire Junction. This connection allowed freight and passenger service to be added to its timber transport. For 40 cents passengers could ride from Empire to Empire Junction where they made the connection with M. & N.E., which ran to Traverse City.

The lumber era was a prosperous time for Empire and the population grew to 700. By the time the village was incorporated in 1895, it boasted Methodist and Catholic churches, a new hotel, two saloons, a newspaper, and several other businesses. Newly arrived immigrants, including many Belgians and Norwegians,

Empire from Empire Bluff No. 1

Dear Friend:
I am home at last
and have been camping
since I came. I suppose you
think I had forgotten you but O. No.
Had a dance here Sat. night,
a ball game Sun. & a marsh-
mellow roast Sun. night.
I wish I might have been
there for that corn roast.
I was in T.C. a week. Had
a dandy time.

Postmarked Empire, 1910,
Mailed to Williamsburg, Michigan

found work in Empire. Most of the Belgians worked in the logging camps and the Norwegians worked in the sawmill. The Belgians settled in Empire, while the Norwegians settled just south of the mill in the area that became known as Norway Town.

In 1906 the first mill burned and was soon rebuilt with a larger and more efficient 16-blade band sawmill. The new mill produced between 15 and 20 million board feet of lumber each year. When a second fire struck the mill in 1917, the timber in the surrounding area was nearly gone and the mill was not rebuilt.

Much of the cutover land was sold for farming. Many acres were planted with apples, peaches, and cherries. By 1910 there were as many as 16,000 cherry trees in the area. Fruit farming became the mainstay of the economy as the lumbering era drew to a close.

Tourism started to increase in the 1920s with the growth in automobile travel. Tourists were drawn to the Empire area for its proximity to the scenic attractions of Glen Lake and Sleeping Bear Dunes. The quaint village of Empire provided shops and services for the increasing number of visitors to the area. In the 1970s the Sleeping Bear Dunes National Lakeshore was established and Empire became the home of the park's Visitors Center.

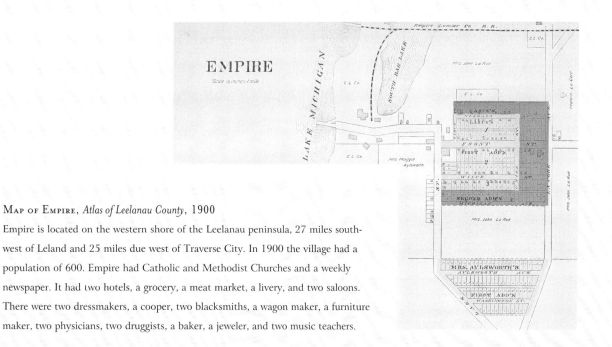

MAP OF EMPIRE, *Atlas of Leelanau County*, 1900

Empire is located on the western shore of the Leelanau peninsula, 27 miles southwest of Leland and 25 miles due west of Traverse City. In 1900 the village had a population of 600. Empire had Catholic and Methodist Churches and a weekly newspaper. It had two hotels, a grocery, a meat market, a livery, and two saloons. There were two dressmakers, a cooper, two blacksmiths, a wagon maker, a furniture maker, two physicians, two druggists, a baker, a jeweler, and two music teachers.

Picturesque Village

One of the most picturesque villages on the entire West Michigan Pike is Empire, with a population of about 800, nestled in a delightful valley in the southwestern corner of Leelanau County. With her electric lighted streets, cement sidewalks, and waterworks, she gives evidence of her enterprising citizens. Empire has university approved schools, churches, banks, commercial and hotel facilities, rail and water transportation, being the terminus of a railroad and on the bank of Lake Michigan, with a beautiful small deep lake just at the shore of the big lake, awaiting only the action of Uncle Sam to turn it into one of the finest and safest of harbors.

The view from the hills on either entrance to the valley is beautiful in the extreme, and many there are of widely traveled folk, who style it the loveliest scene their eyes have ever looked upon.

In the country surrounding are many fine farms and orchards, in fact the largest orchard enterprise in the state is here, as well as one of the finest bearing apple orchards to be found anywhere. The nutritious grasses and the abundance of pure, sparkling spring water, make it also ideal for stock raising.

The fame of this section is also well established as "par excellence" fishing country, with its unsurpassed trout streams, and little lakes full of bass, pickerel, etc.

The real farmer finds his greatest opportunity here; the city dweller, the business man of affairs in search of the ideal country home, need look no further than the Empire territory to find what they have dreamed of, as the place to work out to a successful issue their plans for "back to the land."

— *West Michigan Pike,* 1914

A view of Front Street looking west, circa 1920, shows Nurko and Frazier Dry Goods Store, which carried a full line of clothing including ladies' waists, ready-made skirts, good men's suits, and good working shirts.

Empire Lumber Co. Store

The Empire Lumber Company Store, circa 1915. "Dealers in everything. Cash paid for all kinds of forest products. Choice farming lands for sale cheap." The store was located on the present site of Deering's Market until New Year's of 1927 when fire consumed it.

The Western Hotel

The Western Hotel was built in 1884 as the New European Hotel. It was renamed the Western Hotel by the new owners in 1898. Located on the corner of Niagara and La Rue Streets, it was torn down in 1935. The hotel's letterhead proclaimed it "an ideal place to enjoy your vacation." Located in the best fruit belt in Michigan.

John Fry, General Merchandise

Posing in their new automobile in front of the John Fry General Store is Mr. Fry, seated next to him is his daughter Leota, and in the back seat is Mrs. Fry and their son Al. To the left and behind the store is the home of John La Rue, the first settler in Empire. Circa 1910.

"Storm Hill," Empire

"Storm Hill" was the summer home of Harvey Wilce. Built in 1910, it sat on the top of Storm Hill overlooking the Empire Lumber Company with Lake Michigan and Sleeping Bear Dunes directly behind. The central attraction of the home was a large interior fountain.

Wilce Hill from Front St., Empire

Wilce Hill from Front Street, Empire, Mich.

West end of Front Street showing the Aylesworth Boarding House on the left,

Collins Hardware on the right, and the Wilce home atop Storm Hill.

The Beach, Empire

The Beach, Empire, Mich.

Dear Etta,

This is a card taken close by of Lake Michigan a little to the left of the little town we live in. It is pleasant here in the summer — always a cool breeze from off the lake. I hope that you get strong so that you can come home and be reunited to your family, or better yet come and see us and spend the summer. I would like to see you so would your father. He has gained 11 lbs. since he came up here. When you feel all right let us hear from you again. With lots of wishes I will close.

— Mrs. J.

Postmarked Empire, circa 1915

Mailing address not legible

Friday

Dear Grandma, It is almost noon, have just been down to the lake and it is covered with whitecaps and the water is splashing over the dock. It is awful pretty but I don't want to get very near. It is quite cool this morning. Am having a nice time. I expect you are washing dishes and tending the garden. Don't think of any more. Good bye.

— CV

Postmarked Empire, 1913
Mailed to Ovid, Mich.

8-16-1930
Dear Folks,
Enjoying our stay here very much. Wonderful lake, good bathing and fishing. Scenery grand. Just finished lunch of the fish Dick caught yesterday — the limit in two hours. A neighbor caught a 10 3/4 lb. Mackinaw trout (copper wire fishing) yesterday. We are now going riding again to view more of the sites. Hope all are well as we are.

— Love, Delia

Postmarked Empire, 1930
Mailed to Grand Rapids, Michigan

Sleeping Bear Sand Dunes

The Native Americans had a legend about Sleeping Bear Dunes. They said that long ago a mother bear and her two cubs fled from a forest fire in Wisconsin by swimming across the big lake to Michigan. The mother reached shore first and climbed wearily up a steep bluff to watch and wait for her cubs, but they became exhausted and drowned within sight of land. The mother bear lay grieving, watching the spot where the cubs had drowned. The Great Spirit Manitou in mercy turned the cubs into North and South Manitou Islands, and gently covered the mother bear with sand, forming the dune we call "Sleeping Bear."

The Sleeping Bear Sand Dunes have been called the "Michigan Sahara" because they are one of the few places where it is possible to see nothing but endless sand. They rise sheer from the shore of Lake Michigan 400 feet above the water and stretch from Sleeping Bear Bay on the north to the village of Empire on the south, a distance of five miles. Comprising an area of about 10 square miles, the dunes tower over Glen Lake on the west. They are said to be the largest moving landmass in the country.

"The Bear," as it is popularly called, is made up of gravel and fine white sand that is constantly blown and shifted by the prevailing southwesterly winds. The dunes are also affected to a lesser degree by the northwesterly winds. These opposite forces create the soft, flowing contours of the dune land-scape. The dunes are moving toward Glen Lake at the rate of 2 feet to 6 feet per year, burying trees and vegetation on their way. By looking at old photographs, one can see how much the dunes have changed over the years.

In 1931 the Michigan Department of Conservation acquired 1,545 acres of duneland from the federal government. This was the beginning of the Sleeping Bear State Park project. By 1955 the project boundary was established at more than 2,000 acres. The state recommended that suitable land be purchased as rapidly as feasible. By 1957 the rare scenic beauty and the value of

Dear Norma,

We have a great old time around here. It's beautiful — hiking, swimming, fishing, boating, bicycling, auto trips, etc. Yesterday we went way up to the far end of this peninsular, [*sic*] through Northport, Suttons Bay, etc. Yours truly did all the driving. We were gone all day. Today it is raining and it seems good to get a chance to spend a few hours at our small cottage. Went through the canning factory at Northport.

— Love, Hat

Postmarked Glen Arbor, 1939
Mailed to Grand Rapids, Michigan

the dune ecosystem brought national notice. In 1976 Sleeping Bear Dune State Park, along with D.H. Day State Park, became part of the Sleeping Bear Dunes National Lakeshore.

These mountains of sand are certainly one of Michigan's most dramatic natural wonders. Due to the enterprise of one man, Louis Warnes, they became the scene of one of the most popular tourist attractions of their day. The dune rides were started in 1935 by Louis Warnes and his wife Marion, D.H. Day's youngest daughter. The rides operated for 43 years, using the old D.H. Day General Store as the starting point. The first "dunesmobile" was a 1934 Ford, which took four passengers on a ride from Glen Haven to the crest of the sand dunes and back. The ride cost 25 cents. The venture was so popular that the couple expanded their operation. Louis mapped a trail over the dunes creating a 15-mile ride of unmatched beauty, with breathtaking views of Lake Michigan, the Manitou Islands, and Glen Lake. So many people came that it was necessary to purchase more dunesmobiles.

The first fleet of dunesmobiles were 1937 Fords equipped with oversize balloon tires. The second fleet consisted of ten 1948 Fords, and the third fleet began with ten new 1956 Super 88 Oldsmobiles. The last fleet started with thirteen 1965 modified Ford pickups. Over the years thousands of people experienced the thrills of riding over the dunes in a dunesmobile. The dune rides ended in 1978 and the Warnes' store closed.

Sleeping Bear Stories

The Indians have one story explaining Sleeping Bear and the geologists have another. The Indians say that in the long ago a mother bear and her two cubs, fleeing from a forest fire in Wisconsin, swam across the big lake to the Michigan side. The mother reached shore first and dragged herself wearily up the steep bluff where she lay down to wait for the cubs. But the cubs became exhausted and sank with safety in sight. The mother bear lay there grieving, watching the spot where the cubs drowned. The Great Spirit in mercy turned the cubs into islands — the present North and South Manitous — and covered the mother bear gently with sand, thus forming the dune that gives the region its name.

The story of the geologists is more prosaic but nonetheless strange. They say that the glaciers laid down the great moronic ridge that is the base of the plateau — a ridge of sand mixed with pebbles, boulders, and gravel. The prevailing southwest winds in the course of centuries blew away the top of this ridge for a mile back from the shore until it is now a flat-topped plateau with an average elevation of 400 or more feet above Lake Michigan. The sands flying, drifting before the winds, have left pebbles and cobble behind on the top of the plateau where they have assumed the characteristic appearance and shape of desert stones.

— Stace, *Michigan's Mystic Dunes,* 1939

...The celebrated "Sleeping Bear"...is one of the points of greatest interest in the state. The stretch of sand dunes, reaching from Sleeping Bear Point to Empire, eight miles to the southward, with its wide expanse of ever changing hills and ravines and a sandy surface that is so hard it can be driven upon, is a glorious place for resorters and picnic parties to while away dreamy summer days. From the top of the Bear a beautiful view of Lake Michigan is to be had. On the surface of the waters of this inland sea are seen the many crafts, from the small carriers to the monster six-hundred footers, that carry the traffic produced by an industrious and prosperous people.

— Day, Glen Lake Region, 1911

Sleeping Bear, Sand Dune, Northwest of Traverse City, Mich.

Sleeping Bear Sand Dune, Northwest of Traverse City, Michigan

Sleeping Bear Point is on the west shore of Leelanau County. It is a large mountain of pure white sand that has been accumulating on that point through centuries, washed up by the restless waves of Lake Michigan and thrown upon the beach, where the winds in turn have caught and carried it forward. It is always moving, always growing, for the forces that create it are ever in motion. Sleeping Bear has caught and imprisoned within his clasp, the giant monarchs of the forest that grew along his path. Their tops peer from the summit or along the sides at passersby as though in mute appeal for liberation. But they will never be released for old Sleeping Bear has lain under the spell of an enchanter for centuries and will never waken until some throes of nature arouse him from his sleeping place beside the blue water.

— Waite and Anderson, *Old Settlers*, circa 1918

Sand Ripples, Sleeping Bear Sand Dune

Sand, then sand and still more sand, long stretches, hills, valleys, mile upon mile of sand. None of us had ever seen Mr. and Mrs. Sahara's exhibit of Africa but now we can imagine it without the expense of a trip.

Warning to all and sundry tourists — this is a man's job, or a Boy Scout's, and not for people who use their cars to go up to the neighborhood grocery ...

— Phelps, *Ye Lakes and Hills of Michigan*, circa 1933

Sand Ripples, Sleeping Bear Sand Dune, Glen Haven, Mich.

Sleeping Bear sand dune will be one of the unique resort
and tourist attractions in the lower peninsula, predicted
William H. Loutit of Grand Haven, chairman of the
state conservation commission, after he and members of
the commission made a thorough inspection of the big
dune.

    "The commission is extremely enthusiastic about
the possibilities of the dune as a tourist and resort
attraction," Chairman Loutit stated…"We sincerely
believe that Sleeping Bear will become one of the
unique attractions in the lower peninsula when it
becomes better known."

— *Traverse City Record Eagle*, July 9, 1938

Russel McLaughlin, who is feature writer on the editorial staff of the Detroit News…spent part of last summer in Leelanau County, and this article was a very clever write-up of the interesting spots that he found here. We quote what he had to say about Glen Lake:

The dunes are in constant motion but do not be alarmed at that. There is no danger of one chasing you up the street. The dunes are not far from Glen Lake, which causes its admirers to look scornful when such mudholes as Lake Lucerne or Lake Louise are mentioned by their traveled friends. Glen Lake hasn't much in the way of mountains for its background, but its environment is well supplied with hills and there is a view to the east, which embraces the lake, and many hundred acres of forest land, a great expanse of Lake Michigan, and looking just as if they were suspended in the air, North and South Manitou Islands…

This writer does not set up to be an authority on views, but he has seen some handsome ones in his day, including a great many Earl Carroll choruses, and he declares unhesitatingly that this particular slant on Glen Lake will linger in your memory when inferior spectacles, such as the Rock of Gibralter and Myrna Loy are forgotten.

— *Leelanau Enterprise*, July 11, 1940

Dune Ride a Region Feature

A few years ago Louis Warnes was riding over the sun-scorched beaches of the great Sleeping Bear Dune. The midday heat was unusually severe and his thoroughbred Arabian horse was getting weary. He stopped for a moment on a high bluff overlooking the vast blue expanse of Lake Michigan.

To the left of him reared the vegetation-covered ruggedness of the "Bear." To the west the sun was setting in a blaze of breathtaking splendor. To his right was a rolling desert that folks within a few miles did not know existed. Behind him sand-whipped cedar stumps reared their ghostly forms and the blood red of the sinking sun cast weird shadows across the wind-rippled sand.

He reasoned to himself that there must be some way to show this to the people. Somehow or another he must think of a means of traveling in comfort over the miles of bleak dunes country to bring to the public the grandeur and beauty that was unheralded.

Horses were not the answer. The few mounts he now rented to resorters were being tortured by the miles of rolling sand trails. They were being overworked because of the increasing demand for their services.

Then he found a solution. He bought a second-hand automobile and after a long search found a set of used tires. Those tires were the answer. They were not common tires but balloon type with wide surface tread and low air pressure.

Mapping a trail over the dunes country he created a 15 mile ride of unmatched scenic splendor and glory. Wind-rippled sand, bleak, half-buried forests, deep gullies, all unfolded before the purring advance of the sand treading automobile cruisers. Over the next dune one could well expect to see a tented city with its gaudily robed bedouins and camel caravans.

Then the world heard about this tour. More modern automobiles were added to the caravan until today seven speedy units course the trail from morning until night. Sunset trips like the one that gave the original inspiration remain the leaders in popularity. At Glen Haven, headquarters for the Dunes Rides, you will find the last word in summer fun and splendor.

— Traverse City Record Eagle, June 25, 1940

Splendid Tours

Supervised tours of the Sleeping Bear Dunes are one of the outstanding thrills for the modern visitor. Special cars — equipped with mammoth, low pressure tires — roll modern automobiles over the wind-packed waste. Heat that sometimes crowds the mercury to 120 degrees is tempered by the brisk pace of the cars, and by the swirling currents of air that constantly surge inland from Lake Michigan.

In an effort to preserve the natural beauty of the "Michigan Desert" for the public, the state conservation department has acquired a great portion of the land and turned it into a public park. This action makes it possible for all people at all times to have the rare treat of wandering over a true desert — in a truly desert atmosphere, without the usual discomforts and lengthy preparations attending such an expedition.

— Traverse City Record Eagle, July 4, 1939

SLEEPING BEAR SAND DUNES GLEN HAVEN MICH

TAKING OFF ON A DUNE RIDE   GLEN HAVEN, MICH G2841

Louis Warnes at Glen Haven has stock cars equipped with oversize tires to carry you on his private roads over
Sleeping Bear. He carries you to a sand peak 450 feet above the lake where you have a really awesome view of
Lake Michigan and Glen Lake, easily one of the most beautiful lakes in the country. And those "roads" are nothing
more than trails so you'll find plenty of thrill on them. For the superb thrill, take the moon-
light trip, and you had better make reservations in advance. Mr. and Mrs. Warnes will try to
interest you in spending the night in the open, sleeping on the warm sands by the lake shore.
There are no insects, nothing but sand and water around you and sky above. There's a
serenity about this detachment from the world which you can seldom know.

— McCracken's 1940 Guide to Michigan

Sleeping Bear Scenic Rides
GLEN HAVEN, MICH.

The Original Sand Dune Ride

L. C. WARNES OWNER
PHONE THE WARNES STORE FOR RESERVATIONS

RIDES . . . . . 50c and $1.00

One of summer's great experiences is a ride up and down the almost perpendicular faces of the dunes on a dunesmobile. It is breathtaking.

— *Vacation Days in the Grand Traverse Bay Region*, circa 1949

Dune Scooting — Deserving of first ranking among all Michigan thrills in my opinion are those stomach flipping but entirely safe dune scooter trips being offered near Hart and Glen Haven along the Lake Michigan shore. If anything like them is available anywhere else in the world, I've never heard of it. They don't sound like much — just automobile rides over big sand piles. But don't be fooled. If you don't forget all dignity and yippee like a cowboy before you're half way through, you're an exception.

— *McCracken's 1940 Guide to Michigan*

Dunesmobiles & Girls from Camp Kohanna

Each summer girls from nearby Camp Kohanna enjoyed the dune rides over Sleeping Bear Dunes. As many as
50 girls took the tour at one time in the fleet of giant-tired 1948 Fords converted into "dunesmobiles."

Digging Snow

Passengers were puzzled when their driver stopped the dunesmobile and shoveled about four feet down in the sand and uncovered white, packed snow. They were amazed at the buried snow, especially when their visit was on a hot, blistering day. The explanation for this phenomenon was that snowdrifts toward the end of winter were gradually covered with sand, which acted as an insulator throughout the hottest summer.

Ski on Sand

If you want to try the comparatively new sport of summer skiing, bring along your equipment. With a steep sand dune, your bathing suit, and a pair of skis, you can put in a novel afternoon skiing down the sand. It is much slower than snow skiing but with a dune of a proper pitch, you can get about as much speed as you want unless you are an expert.

— McCracken's 1940 Guide to Michigan

"Says Sleeping Bear will disappear in 30 years"

Sand Dune, Once 150 Now 86 Feet High, Worn Down by Climbers, Erosion

According to a Kansas State University professor, Sleeping Bear sand dune, one of Michigan's great tourist attractions, will be "gone" in about 30 years.

The professor, who claims to have been studying the formation since 1928, was quoted by the Associated Press in a news broadcast…His name is Frank C. Gates.

Professor Gates stated that Sleeping Bear, said to be the world's largest moving sand dune, "is going the way of all sand dunes, and might be level in 20 or 30 years."

"Tourists tramping over the dunes cause a lot of erosion," he says, "and constant winds from across Lake Michigan do the rest. Now only 86 feet high, the dunes once rose 150 feet into the air."

Scientists have pretty definitely determined that Sleeping Bear is a heap of glacial dirt (moraine) covered with sand; that Glen Lake was once part of Lake Michigan; and that sand pushing down from the dune some day will cover what is now referred to as little Glen Lake.

Indian legend, on the other hand, proclaims that Sleeping Bear really is a huge bear which once escaped from a Wisconsin forest fire and that North and South Manitou Islands are her cubs, who became exhausted in the swim and drowned in Lake Michigan. When the last white man has disappeared, the legend continues, the Sleeping Bear and her two cubs will awaken and be reunited.

Right now it looks as though science might out-run legend in the race with time.

— Leelanau Enterprise, September 16, 1954

Unique Experience

Exciting automobile excursion into strange, secluded desert land set between beautiful Glen Lake and Lake Michigan. Nowhere is there an experience exactly like these dune rides. It is a brief safari into the African Desert without the heat. It is a 19 square mile expanse of unspoiled and untamable natural beauty, where sunsets are spectacles of rare beauties and Lake Michigan is majestic in its every mood. No ordinary cars can dare the shifting sands of Sleeping Bear. All cars are late models equipped with specially built over-size tires, the guides are competent and courteous, and can answer your questions about the Dunes and surrounding area.

— *Sleeping Bear Dunesmobile Scenic Rides,* circa 1959

Dune Climb

It is grand up here. Water is warm. Would like to stay up here longer. We climbed these sand dunes in our bare feet. Had to stop often but could slide down in no time.

— Blossom

Postmarked Traverse City, circa 1962
Mailed to Flint, Michigan

The Original Dune Ride

In 1935 Louis C. Warnes equipped a car with a special motor and giant tires for personal pleasure trips into the vast sand lands near his home. Friends begged him to take passengers. Soon he added other cars and trained drivers. Now a fleet of safe, comfortable new super 88 Oldsmobile convertibles is kept busy each day from the latter part of May until October 1st. Travel editors have "discovered" the Sleeping Bear dune, largest hill of live, shifting sand in the United States. Cars leave at frequent intervals from the Sleeping Bear Gift Shop at Glen Haven, located on M-209 on Lake Michigan. The "dunesmobile" ride is the only complete tour of the dunes and is operated under lease and supervision of the Michigan Conservation Department.

— Sleeping Bear Dunesmobile Scenic Rides, circa 1959

Hi Dear,
Got up here Friday at 6.
Went for a Dunes Ride yesterday and fishing this afternoon on a small lake. No luck! Going again tomorrow to a different lake.
Good weather.

— Love, Rich

Postmarked Glen Arbor, 1965
Mailed to Grand Rapids, Michigan

Each year thousands of visitors enjoyed dunesmobile rides on the Sleeping Bear Dunes.
The rides were one of the area's biggest tourist attractions and people came from all over
the country to see the spectacular sights from the top of the dunes.

Glen Haven

Glen Haven is located on the shore of Lake Michigan, two and one-half miles west of Glen Arbor, 30 miles southwest of Northport, and an equal distance northwest of Traverse City.

Glen Haven got its start in 1857 when C.C. McCarty built a sawmill on the Lake Michigan shore two miles west of Glen Arbor. Nearby he built a small hotel which he called the Sleeping Bear House, but later changed the name to the Sleeping Bear Inn. Near the hotel McCarty built a dock, which provided a sheltered spot and deepwater access for the many vessels passing through the Manitou Passage.

Many of these ships were owned by the Northern Transit Company. The shipping company needed a stable source of cordwood to supply its fleet. The timber in the Glen Haven area supplied that need. In 1878 the Northern Transit Company acquired the dock and the property comprising the village of Glen Haven. David H. Day was sent from Ogdensburg as the company agent in Glen Haven.

By the time Day arrived in 1878, Glen Haven had a population of 50 inhabitants, a general store, a hotel, a sawmill, a flour mill, and a blacksmith shop. Day was to play the central role in Glen Haven's history. By 1885 he had purchased most of the Northern Transit Company's property, including the village of Glen Haven, and went into business for himself. D.H. Day and Company engaged in lumbering, general merchandising, and for a short time owned the steamers *Lawrence* and *Champlain*. Day bought a sawmill on the west end of Little Glen Lake and set up his operations. When a neighboring sawmill, the J.O. Nessen Mill at Glen Arbor, was torn down in 1907, Day bought its locomotive and steel rails. He ran a tramway between his Little Glen sawmill and the dock at Glen Haven, where the lumber was stacked for shipping.

In the 1890s Day was a leader in the movement to provide a means of protecting shipping interests from losses in the Manitou Passage. In 1901 funds were approved for two U.S. Life-Saving Stations. One was built at Sleeping Bear Point and the other on South Manitou Island. In 1915 the U.S. Life-

Saving Service was absorbed by the U.S. Coast Guard. Drifting sand and shoreline erosion forced the Sleeping Bear station to be moved in 1931. It was relocated one-half mile east of the original site, closer to Glen Haven.

David H. Day was a pioneer in reforestation. Day replanted trees in the tracts that had been cutover. He knew that the forest would renew itself and within 50 years the second-growth timber would be ready to harvest. He also left large tracts of forest undisturbed so that the virgin timber would be preserved. By 1910 Day owned more than 5,000-forested acres with tracts of birch, elms, maples, oaks, and pines. His farsighted logging practices kept his operation going until 1923, long after other mills in the area ceased running.

Day planted 1,000 cherry trees in a tract cleared of stumps. He later went on to establish the Glen Haven Canning Company, which canned and shipped fruit and cider to various Great Lake ports. He also built a modern farm and named it "Oswegatchie" after the area in New York State where his father was born. His 400-acre farm produced fruit, hay, corn, livestock and dairy products, and Day was very proud of his herd of fine Holstein cattle. The beautiful farmhouse and barn are a still a well-known landmark in the Sleeping Bear Dunes area.

Many visitors to the area are familiar with the name of D.H. Day because of the campground that bears his name. In 1920 Day was appointed the first commissioner of the State Parks Commission. His first gesture was to donate a 32-acre site, which became the D.H. Day State Park. The property included 700 feet of Lake Michigan shore, shifting sand dunes, and heavy growths of pine and juniper. This was the first park acquired by the State Parks Commission and writings from that time refer to it as "State Park Number 1."

....

Map of Glen Haven, *Atlas of Leelanau County*, 1900
Glen Haven is located on Sleeping Bear Bay 20 miles southwest of Leland and 30 miles northwest of Traverse City. In 1900 Glen Haven had a population of 125. It had a general store, a sawmill, a hotel, a carpenter, two blacksmiths, and a millwright.

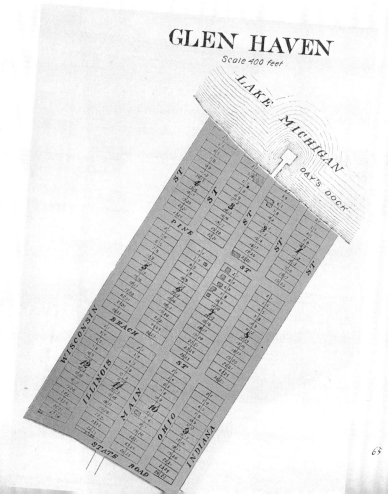

GLEN HAVEN
Scale 400 feet

David Henry Day was rightfully called the "King David" of Leelanau. He is the one person most responsible for the development of the region. He owned the D.H. Day General Store and the Sleeping Bear Inn in Glen Haven. To better accommodate tourists, Day renovated the Sleeping Bear Inn in the mid-1920s. For 19 years he was president of the West Michigan Development Bureau, which promoted West Michigan's agricultural and industrial potential. Day was also an ardent advocate of good roads. He was a county road commissioner for 10 years and county director for the West Michigan Pike Association for several years. Day staged auto rallies in Glen Haven as part of the annual West Michigan Pike tours. He was instrumental in building the road from Empire to Glen Haven, which later became a state trunk line.

In 1922, D.H. Day sold a large tract of land to a real estate broker, who named the development the Day Forest Estates. The centerpiece of the development was Alligator Hill, which is situated between Lake Michigan and Glen Lake. A group of businessmen, including Day, had an ambitious plan to develop the Day Forest Estates into an exclusive summer resort. They had hopes that it would become the permanent summer home of the president of the United States. An 18-hole golf course was built, an airstrip site cleared, and roads into the property were opened. A scenic road was built leading to the site of the proposed clubhouse. A polo field and tennis courts were planned. Ski and toboggan slides, ice-skating and iceboating promised to make Glen Lake the Lake Placid of the Midwest. The building sites, all with scenic views, were laid out with five-acre minimum lots. With the arrival of the Great Depression in 1929 plans came to a halt, and the ambitious venture failed, although the Day Forest Golf Course did later operate for several years.

By the late 1940s the Day Forest property was in the hands of the Theron Goodspeed estate, which was holding it for a suitable buyer. When the Michigan Conservation Department's option to purchase the property expired in July 1949, a group of Glen Lake residents tried unsuccessfully to raise the $100,000 purchase price. In 1950 Pierce Stocking, a Cadillac lumberman, purchased

1,700 acres of the Day Forest Estates. He opened his private Sleeping Bear Dunes Park in the late 1960s. He built a scenic road through the property and charged $3.00 per car for visitors to travel the 14-mile road. In the late 1970s the National Park Service acquired the Pierce Stocking property for the Sleeping Bear Dunes National Lakeshore. The Pierce Stocking Drive is one of the park's most popular attractions.

By the mid-1970s the National Park Service had acquired the village of Glen Haven and most of the surrounding properties as part of Sleeping Bear Dunes National Lakeshore. Some of the early buildings still stand including the D.H. Day General Store, the Sleeping Bear Inn, the Glen Haven Canning Company, and the U.S. Life-Saving Service/Coast Guard Station. The village of Glen Haven is an Historic District on the National Register of Historic Places.

Glen Haven with boat at dock

The fine passenger steamers Illinois *and* City of Charlevoix, *of the Northern Michigan Transportation Company of Chicago, make regular stops at Glen Haven, which is in close proximity of the different resorts on Glen Lake. At Glen Haven, there is a good hotel for the accommodation of tourists, coming and going, and which also has good accommodations for guests; and near which is the celebrated Sleeping Bear — a wonderful formation of nature. Parties wishing to visit the celebrated Manitou Islands can from this point get good boat service three times per week.*

— Beauty Spots in Leelanau, 1901 Souvenir

Opposite Page: Store and Post Office, Glen Haven
The D. H. Day General Store was the center of life in Glen Haven for several generations. Local lumberjacks and dock-hands got their supplies and mail there and caught up on local gossip. After Day's death the store was operated by Louis and Marion Warnes, D. H. Day's youngest daughter. It was the starting point for the Sleeping Dune Dunesmobile Scenic Rides from the mid 1930s to 1978.

Six Steamers Call Each Week
Glen Haven made colorful by Lake Michigan traffic

Of all the ports on the call of the Michigan Transit Company steamers there is none that takes on more summer color than Glen Haven, which serves as a distributing point for Lake Michigan passenger traffic for Glen Lake and other regions.

Glen Haven has six boats a week, the "Manitou" calling four times and the "Puritan" twice. Northbound Glen Haven has the "Manitou" Tuesday morning at 7:00 and Saturday morning at 9:30 and the "Puritan" at 12:30 Wednesday afternoon. Southbound the "Manitou" stops at 6:00 Thursday evening, and the same hour on Sunday evening, and the "Puritan" at 11:00 Friday morning.

Nearly seventy-five per cent of the traffic on the "Manitou's" weekend trip out of Chicago is for Glen Haven cottages, and tourists disembarking at the Glen Haven docks for Northport, Traverse City, the sundry Glen Lake resorts and even the resorts on the other side of Grand Traverse Bay.

The village presents a picturesque appearance on Sunday evenings when cars from miles around are parked near the docks for the farewell to the weekend visitors. The service between Chicago and Glen Haven affords nearly two days at the Grand Traverse resorts between Friday and Monday, the Chicagoans leaving home Friday evening and being returned in time for business Monday morning.

— Traverse City Record Eagle, July 31, 1926

Sleeping Bear Inn at edge of Lake Michigan

Hotel, Glen Haven, Mich.

Solidly set down at Lake Michigan's edge and facing the lake in two directions is Sleeping Bear Inn, located at Glen Haven near the Sleeping Bear Dune, from which the Inn takes its name.

The Inn, constructed many years ago, and in as good condition now as it was then, has been completely modernized, with every convenience for its guests.

During the day the cool breezes from Lake Michigan fan across the wide porches, cool, but not to the point of being chilly. And when storm clouds are hanging low in the sky and Lake Michigan lashes at the white sand of the beach, guests may gather in the cozy lounge before a brightly burning fire in the fireplace, forgetting the angry wind that is whining outside unable to penetrate to the warm comfort within.

And on days when the wind is fresh and strong, while the sky is clear, a battle with the proud waves of Lake Michigan is welcomed by strong swimmers, and the white sand of the wide beach is an inviting toaster ready to change the white backs and arms to a beautiful brown. For guests who dislike the boisterous Lake Michigan combers, Glen Lake is but a few minutes drive from the Inn.

And the appetite worked up in strenuous play is plentifully satisfied at a well-laden dinner table. Home cooking is a specialty of the Sleeping Bear Inn.

Golf, tennis, fishing, bridle paths and all sports are ready for the restless sportsman. Fishing on Glen Lake is enjoyed by all.

Rooms at the Inn are cool and inviting, and the extra blanket provided is often needed at Sleeping Bear, while inland Michigan swelters in heat reflected from the pavement and the ground. Mrs. Amanda Bunch is a cordial and charming hostess, always ready to help.

Rates are reasonable, with a proper rate reduction for children. Overnight guests are accommodated.

— *Traverse City Record Eagle,* June 30, 1937

Glen Haven Cannery has had Busy Season

The cherry canning factory at Glen Haven has just closed what is no doubt the most productive season since it began its operation. It is estimated that over a million pounds of cherries have been canned.

The factory is operated independently and has played a big part in helping to take care of the region's enormous cherry crop. Its location makes it accessible to a large portion of the cherry belt.

— Leelanau Enterprise, August 14, 1930

Glen Haven proves that Mich is also on the map for beauty spots. It is wonderful here.

—Ted

Postmarked Empire, circa 1920
Mailed to Detroit, Michigan

No. 12-4   Glen Haven Harbor from Sleeping Bear Dune, Michigan

Coast Guard Station, Sleeping Bear Point

The U.S. Life Saving Service built two identical stations to keep watch over the Manitou Passage. The first was built in 1901 at Sleeping Bear Point near Glen Haven, and the second station was finished in 1902 on South Manitou Island. In 1915 the U.S. Life Saving Service was absorbed by the U.S. Coast Guard. Drifting sand and shoreline erosion forced the Sleeping Bear station to be moved in 1931 to the present site at Glen Haven, one-half mile east of the original site

No. 12-6   Coast Guard Station, Sleeping Bear Point, Glen Haven, Mich.

Glen Haven, Mich.

The D. H. Day State Park: *Lying far in the north on the Leelanau peninsula, projecting out the into Lake Michigan with Grand Traverse Bay on the east and meeting the shores of Lake Michigan on the west, but a few miles north of Traverse City is located the D. H. Day State Park. This is on state highway M-22, which joins trunk line M-11 near Manistee. The site contains thirty-three acres and is famous for the magnificent height of its sand dunes. There is no better bathing beach in all of Michigan. Scattered throughout the park will be found tall Norway and white pines and a few sturdy oaks.*

The entire surrounding territory, in addition to the park itself, is one of great scenic beauty and no doubt this will be one of the favorite resorts for campers and tourists. Traversing the center of this park will be found an old Indian trail that is rich in legend and myth.

This was the first State Park established by the people.

— The Parks of the People, circa 1924

Between Glen Haven and Glen Arbor, and also situated on Lake Michigan, is the David H. Day Estate Park, outstanding in Michigan's splendid system of camping places. A store supplies the wants of the tourists, while stoves, well water, playground equipment and a fine bathing beach prove an attractive calling card. Fascinating hikes through the surrounding woodland and along the shore provide many happy hours of unusual and profitable forms of recreation for campers.

— Traverse City Record Eagle, June 30, 1934

Lake Tabors Cottage - State Park - Glen Haven Mich.

State Park and Tourist Camp, Glen Haven, Mich.

State Park and
Tourist Camp, Glen Haven

D. H. Day State Park

A great many campers are taking advantage of the natural beauties of the State Park here. Facilities for campers have been carefully worked out, and the construction of camping sites, outdoor stoves and playgrounds with equipment make the park an attractive place to stay. Unusual care has been taken to keep things as clean and sanitary as possible.

— *Leelanau Enterprise,* July 17, 1930

Glen Haven State Park 7/28/27

Came up here yesterday after spending a few days at Interlochen State Park. This is a beautiful country. Glen Lake looks like some of the pictures of the lakes in Ireland. Having the finest weather, but no fish. Hope you had a nice time on your trip

— Floyd

Postmarked Empire, 1927
Mailed to Freeland, Michigan

Bath Houses, Michigan State Park #1 Glen Haven, Mich.

State Parks had Many Visitors during Past Season

State Parks of Michigan have proven very popular with tourists during the past summer season according to figures given out by the State Conservation Department.

Among the finest parks in the state is the D. H. Day Park at Glen Haven. This park occupies a tract near Lake Michigan and was donated to the state by the late David H. Day. During the past season this park was visited by 44,891 persons. The Traverse City State Park in Grand Traverse county had 27,403 visitors.

— *Leelanau Enterprise*, November 11, 1929

"Oswegatchie" Farm, Glen Haven

At the northeast corner of the lake (Glen Lake), is the D. H. Day sawmill and Oswegatchie Farm. The latter is one of the best kept-up farms in the state. The buildings are modern and of generous proportions. The Holstein herd numbers over sixty head, there are fifty acres of alfalfa, and several large orchards. The sawmill at the west end of the lake is connected with Glen Haven by a steam railroad. At the village there is a gasoline station, a blacksmith shop, and general store, at which all the things that the tourist is likely to need, may be had.

— *West Michigan Pike*, 1914

LAKE MICHIGAN FROM DAY FOREST ESTATE. NEAR TRAVERSE CITY. MICH

Reforestation Value Proved by Day Project

Long before either the state or his competitors fully recognized the need of putting something back in place of the timber which was being harvested. D. H. Day, wealthy Glen Haven lumberman, started his reforestation project on Glen Lake. Today Mr. Day has a forest of hardwood fifty years old, the biggest project of its kind in the state.

Mr. Day reforested simply by selecting a well situated tract of land from which the virgin timber had been cut, keeping fire out and permitting young trees to come along as nature intended they should. All Mr. Day assures these youngsters is protection from fire. This is all they ask and the size of the trees in this fifty year old woods is evidence that reforestation on a big scale is practical.

This is not a private place, this vast stretch of woodland, but is open to the public. Long, shady paths wind through the forest, following no definite line, but leading the explorer on and on until the forest limit is reached. This alone is worth a trip to Glen Lake.

— Traverse City Record Eagle, July 31, 1926

Clearing Roadway, Day Forest Estate

A picturesque crew of "jacks" from the lumber camps of Kalkaska County are now busy putting in twelve miles of roads through the 1,800 acres of the Day Forest Estates. That work and a few other activities…will take up the remainder of the present season, further development activities to proceed in the spring.

— Traverse City Record Eagle, July 19, 1927

Clearing Roadway, Day Estate, Glen Lake, Michigan.

Day Forest Estates are Now Open for Inspection

The Day Forest Estates on beautiful Glen Lake, Leelanau County, Michigan, announces that due to the insistent requests of many wealthy summer visitors to the project, a number of choice estates, with charming vistas, were opened for personal inspection and selecting on August 10th.

A few of these estates are located contiguous to the sporty 18-hole golf course, with a marvelous view of the majestic Lake Michigan, while several estates overlook Glen Lake with its ever changing iridescent waters, all offering locations for summer country homes with unexcelled natural beauty and being serviced from the twelve miles of forest trails traversing the entire 1,700 acre development.

The Field Office on the property announces daily visitors number into hundreds, coming from all sections of the United States, to view the grandeur and charm of this magnificent natural setting, being so ideally embellished for man's habitation and suited perfectly for his summer country home.

The Day Forest Estates…will undoubtedly become the "finest in America" of developments of its type and its successful completion will bring tremendous prestige to all of Western Michigan in its efforts to fulfill the slogan "The Playground of the Nation."

— *Traverse City Record Eagle*, August 15, 1929

GLEN LAKE
Leelanau County

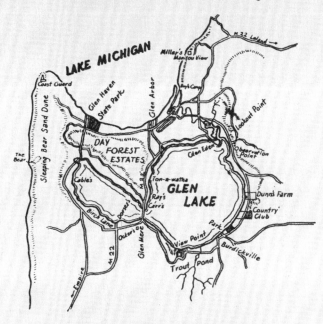

SETTING OF THE
Day Forest Estates
THE MOST ELABORATE RESORT DEVELOPMENT IN MICHIGAN

And Summer Homes of Gene and Glen famous radio entertainers, Jake and Lena.

— *Glen Lake, Leelanau County, Michigan*, 1931

Gateway to Day Estates

Offers Forests for Presidents

Day Estates to go to Congress as Likely Site

Michigan may become the permanent summer capital of the nation. Day Forest Estates, admittedly America's foremost northern resort project, will be offered to the United States government as a site for the permanent summer capital and White House ...

Located near the nation's center of population, between Glen Lake, Leelanau County, one of the most beautiful inland lakes on the continent, according to many eminent authorities, and the scenic Lake Michigan coast, in the vicinity of the Manitou Islands and historic Sleeping Bear Point, the far famed Day forests are undoubtedly the best site available today for the summer White House of the world's greatest nation. The superb water setting, the great natural forests, and the Riviera climate of Western Michigan, tempered by prevailing westerly winds over Lake Michigan combine to make this site without a peer.

The Day Forest comprises 1,800 acres on a rise that reaches a height of 500 feet, with the blue of Lake Michigan to the West and North and the sparkling waters of Glen Lake to the South and East. The summer capital would be a landmark visible for many miles over Lake Michigan, the only one of the inland seas entirely owned by the United States, over the land, or from the air. No capital in the world would have a more imposing position.

— *Traverse City Record Eagle,* July 19, 1927

DRAWING OF CLUBHOUSE

Day Forest Estates on Beautiful Glen Lake, circa 1928

Clubhouse, To Be Completed During 1929.

D. H. Day holding a newspaper promoting Day Forest Estates circa 1927. A group of businessmen planned an exclusive resort on the 1,800-acre Alligator Hill, which is situated between Glen Lake and Lake Michigan. Plans called for one of the finest 18-hole golf courses in America, a beach and tennis club on the Lake Michigan shore, bridle paths, a polo field, an airstrip, and a rebuilt dock at Glen Arbor to accommodate yachts. A proposal to make the Day Estates the permanent summer home of the U.S. president was brought before a special session of congress in 1928, but nothing came of the proposal. When the stock market crashed in 1929, plans for the Day Forest Estates were halted.

Plat Showing Approximate Size and Location of the 120 Estates.

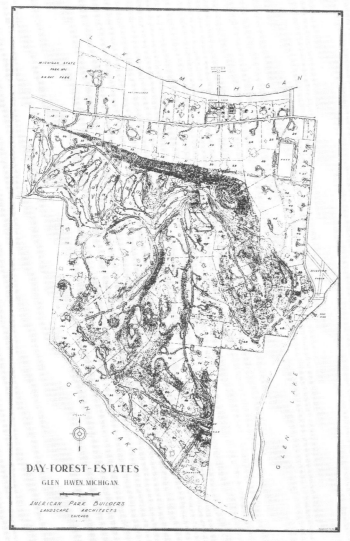

For Complete Information, address:

Day Forest Estates

J. B. WAGNER, *General Manager*
Realtor   Cadillac, Michigan

B. R. HENDEL, *Sales Manager*
Realtor   Manistee, Mich.

Day Forest Golf Course under construction. This course was the centerpiece of the Day Forest Estates.

— *Day Forest Estates on Beautiful Glen Lake,* circa 1928

Day Forest Estate Golf Course

Cut out of twenty-five hundred acres of timberland,
the Day Forest Estate Golf Course offers eighteen holes
of the finest type of challenge to golfers in Leelanau
County. The course has long had a reputation of being
particularly difficult and has been an incentive to
golfers to try their skill on its rolling fairways.

The grounds are laid out on beautifully wooded
hills overlooking Lake Michigan, with the famous
Manitou Islands in the distance, and are truly one of the
scenic spots of the North.

— *Traverse City Record Eagle,* July 30, 1933

ADVERTISEMENT — DAY FOREST GOLF COURSE
— *Traverse City Record Eagle,* 1935

A View on the D.H. Day Golf Course W4

Day Forest is Lovely Eighteen-Hole Lay-out

Long, rolling fairways, and well watered springy greens tempt every golfer who passes through the Glen Lake region, and near the beautiful 18-hole golf course at Day Forest Estate, overlooking Glen Lake and Lake Michigan. Hewn out of hillsides, through forests of tall trees the Day Estate Course is undoubtedly one of the most beautiful as well as one of the sportiest courses in the country.

The course, which cost $330,000 is managed by B. R. Hendel, who is operating at moderate green fees.

At the top of a lofty hill, in the midst of the magnificent Day Forest is located the "Pro" house, and beside it the first tee and fairway, stretching down through a tree lined corridor. Although the trees bordering the fairways, and the rolling hills present hazards, the fairways are wide and greens are large, offering all players a chance to battle with some success against par.

A short distance from the "Pro" house is the parking space, a clearing in the trees from which is obtained a view of scenic grandeur unsurpassed. From the great height of the course, the Manitou Islands several miles off shore in Lake Michigan seem close, and even the Fox Islands, many miles away are seen clearly.

The deep, deep blue of Lake Michigan, and the water-tempered breeze which plays over the hills at all times are both invigorating and restful.

On all sides, extending down to the very shore of Lake Michigan, a mile away, are the tall trees and sloping hills of the vast Day Forest Estates.

The course, itself, is a marvel of engineering and landscaping. Each fairway is broad and rolling, and each has its own problems to be solved by the skillful golfer. Some of the best golfers in Michigan and neighboring states have played the course, and pronounced it one of the sportiest and the most beautiful they have ever played.

An excellent watering system keeps each fairway and green in perfect condition, and golfers drive for miles to play the Day course, while tourists drive up the long, winding road to the summit, for the marvelous view which it affords.

— Traverse City Record Eagle, June 30, 1937

Glen Lake Region

Glen Lake is located in the southwestern part of Leelanau County. It stretches from one to three miles wide and is seven miles long, covering about 7,680 acres. Glen Lake was once called Bear Lake, because of the many bears prowling the heavy forests along its shore. In 1858 the name was changed to Glen Lake. Although it is actually one large lake, the two bodies of water separated at the narrows are referred to as "Big Glen" and "Little Glen." Glen Lake abounds in fish — including bass, lake trout, northern pike, and perch. It was first stocked by the state of Michigan in 1893 with bass, trout, and pike and its early reputation as a fishermen's paradise continues to this day.

The first settlement on the shore of Glen Lake was Burdickville. William Burdick came to the area in 1864 and built a sawmill and gristmill. John Helm followed in 1867 and established a general store. Other settlers soon followed. The Helm store and post office were the center of community life on the east shore of the lake. Although Burdick's sawmill burned in 1869, other sawmills were built. Lumbering operations continued and the cutover lands were used by farmers for raising potatoes and root vegetables.

As lumbering declined, farming and tourism began to have an impact on the area's economy. In 1911 D.H. Day issued a promotional booklet, *Glen Lake Region*, offering farmlands for sale, with the "object being to show the possibilities of Glen Lake as a 'summer land,' and to point out that the business of providing for resorters is fast becoming one of great importance in that it furnishes profitable markets for the products of the farms..."[1] By 1911 there were already six established resorts on the shores of Glen Lake.

Gregory's Resort, later known as Tonyawatha, and then Old Orchard Inn, was located on the western shore of Big Glen, just south of Glen Arbor. Ray's Resort was situated near the narrows. The Cedar Springs Lodge was built on a commanding spot on the north side of Little Glen. Cold Springs Resort was located on the south shore of Little Glen. It later became known as Ocker's, then the Glen Lake Manor. Kenwood was also located on the southern shore. It had been a farmhouse, but was enlarged to accommodate summer guests. Another early resort was Asher Atkinson's, located on the southeastern shore at Burdickville.

---

[1] D.H. Day, *Glen Lake Region* Traverse City: Herald and Record Co., 1911 page 2.

The wide sandy beaches and magnificent vistas of Glen Lake continued to attract resorters to the area. More resorts began operation including Dunn's Farm, Krull's Resort, the Glen Eden Hotel, and MacDonald's Resort. As more visitors came to Glen Lake, more accommodations were needed. In the 1930s tourist cabins and cottages sprang up along the Glen Lake shore. These included the Pioneer Cabins, Little Glenn's Log Cabins, Holden's Tourist Cabins, and Carr's Cabin Camp. The postwar years brought a building boom to the Glen Lake area. More rental cottages were built including Scotty's Haven, Glenview Resort, Red Rooster Cottages, Hillview, Glen Craft, and Garsides Resort.

Recognition of Glen Lake's beauty goes back many years. In 1926 the *Traverse City Record Eagle* reported that *National Geographic Magazine* had called Glen Lake one of the five most beautiful lakes in the world. That quotation from *National Geographic* has not been substantiated, but it has taken on a life of its own. Variations have appeared for years. Glen Lake has been called "the most beautiful lake in the nation"; "the second most beautiful lake in the world"; and the "third most beautiful lake in the world." Variations on the theme have persisted over the years. Glen Lake has also been called the "Switzerland of Michigan."

From the steep hills that surround Glen Lake there are scenic spots that have magnificent views. Inspiration Point, Miller Hill and St. Pierre, and Top of the World have attracted sightseers for years. Another attraction was the Old Settlers Park on the shores of Glen Lake, the site of an annual "homecoming" picnic that has been going on since 1893. A mile down the road was the location of the Glen Lake Country Club, organized in 1921 with its first season of golf in 1925. For 10 years this course competed with the Day Forest Golf Course. In the 1930s snipe racing on Glen Lake became popular and regattas were organized by some of the resorters. More people became involved and it was decided that a meeting place was needed. A group of local sailors organized the Glen Lake Yacht Club and a clubhouse was built in 1941.

As more people came to recognize the value of Glen Lake's scenic beauty, more cottages and summer homes were built along its shores. The old resorts are gone and few rental establishments remain, but with Sleeping Bear Dunes National Lakeshore so close to Glen Lake, thousands of visitors have now seen "the most beautiful lake in the nation."

FISHERMAN AT THE NARROWS, circa 1920

The Narrows Bridge, Glen Lake

Two views of the wooden bridge across Glen Lake at the narrows. This first bridge across the narrows was proposed in 1901 and completed in 1905. It was at this point that people to began to refer to "Big Glen" and "Little Glen." The wooden bridge was used until 1939 when it was replaced with a low concrete bridge.

Glen Lake

The Narrows on Glen Lake,

Glen Lake Region from Grand View Hill.

The view from Miller Hill was as spectacular in 1886 as it was in this 1930s postcard.

From an eminence about 400 feet high, two or three miles inland from Glen Arbor, on the northeast side of Glen Lake, can be seen one of the most beautiful and varied landscapes to be witnessed in any country, and one which is well worthy of the pencil of an artist. The view is toward the west, and it should be taken when the sky is clear and the atmosphere is pervaded by that softened haze which fuses the sharper angles of the landscape and throws over it a thin veil of inscrutable vagueness. From our hill summit we look down on the tops of the trees which cover the plain immediately fronting us. On the left is a portion of Glen Lake, its nearer shore concealed by the forest, and the remoter one exposing a white and pebbly margin, from which the verdant hills beyond rise hundreds of feet above the watery mirror in which their forms are so clearly fashioned. In front of us the green hills separate Glen Lake from Lake Michigan, and conceal from view the desert sand fields of Sleeping Bear. Not completely, however, for the naked and glistening slopes of the northern slope stretch out to view beyond the forest covered ridge, and embrace the placid harbor which struggles through the intercepting foliage, and blends with the boundless expanse of the great lake still beyond. Farther off in the midst of the water, rises the green outline of the South Manitou Island, bearing on its head a glistening cap of sand. Still farther to the right rises the form of the North Manitou, which seems to try hiding itself behind the towering bluff of North Unity, that guards the entrance to the harbor from the north. Two little lakes nestle in the rich woodland that spreads its verdure between us and the harbor, screening themselves like wood nymphs behind the thick foliage which half conceals their charms. It is doubtful whether a scene superior to this one exists in the country.

— Winchell, Grand Traverse Region: a Report on the Geological and Industrial Resources, 1866

THE NARROWS, GLEN LAKE, NEAR TRAVERSE CITY, MICH.

Glen Lake

Glen Lake gives the vacationist his first glimpse of the charm of the real northern country, that indefinable something that is in the air, and which draws summer visitors in ever-increasing numbers to this beautiful section each year. Here the sky is bluer blue and the hills a greener green, and as the country becomes more upland, the spell of the north is revealed.

— Traverse City Record Eagle, July 31, 1926

Most Beautiful Lake in Nation

Glen Lake Recognized as one of the World's Five Prettiest Spots

Glen Lake! Need one say more? To say Glen Lake in the middle west is the same as saying the Alps in Switzerland, Atlantic City in the east and Palm Beach in the south.

Glen Lake's reputation as the most beautiful body of inland water in the United States is recognized. Story and picture have very thoroughly presented Glen Lake's beauty to the world and little more can be said or pictured to promote this beautiful lake.

Cupped between high forest clad hills, which hold the blue lake as though in the gigantic palm of nature, the crystal water mirrors the forests, branch for branch and leaf for leaf. When the lake slumbers peacefully one may almost reach the cool depths with the naked eye, so clear is the water, but when the breeze comes dancing across from Lake Michigan, the surface scintillates like a field of gems, breaking onto billions of sparkling points.

Of Glen Lake Prof. Laphan of Columbia University said, through the columns of the National Geographic Magazine, *"Glen Lake is one of the five most beautiful lakes in the world." Three of the others were in Europe and the only other one on the American continent was Lake Louise, Canada.*

But Glen Lake is not the only attraction of the Glen Lake district, although it is the centerpiece. Nearby is Sleeping Bear, that picturesque landmark by which sailors of the lakes have charted their courses since the lake navigation started. It is a tremendously big sand dune, covered with juniper and from Lake Michigan it appears as a big sleeping bear. From the top of the dune one gets an unrivaled view of Lake Michigan and the islands.

This is but one of the natural features which makes the Glen Lake district interesting and intriguing. People never spend one summer in the region. If they come once they return again and again, summer after summer, lured by its greenness, its coolness and its loveliness.

— Traverse City Record Eagle, July 31, 1926

Right: ADVERTISEMENT — GLEN LAKE REGION
— "Vacation Handbook and Fisherman's Guide, Leelanau County," Leelanau Enterprise, 1939

THE
Glen Lake Region
Beckons to You
With Its
Sand Dunes
Sleeping Bear
Crystal River
Glen Lake
Day Forest
Golf Course
D. H. Day Park
Coast Guard Station
Cherry Cannery
Excellent Fishing
Where to GO

Glen Arbor Township

Gilbert Warnes, Supervisor   Cloys Rader, Township Clerk
William LaVance, Treasurer
J. K. Stock and Charlie Miller, Justices of the Peace
—14—

"There are no sneezes in Glen Lake breezes."

A drive through the forests over miles and miles of perfect gravel roads devoid of heavy traffic, over hills, across crystal streams where the wiley brook trout are jumping for white millers, you drive to an elevation overlooking Glen Lake or Lake Michigan, the sun setting, a few clouds have gathered to create a sunset picture for you that no human can hope to paint.

Call it a day if you wish, but, if the family desires further pleasure, it is but a pleasant drive over perfect road to Traverse City, where the latest Talkies are shown.

— Glen Lake, Leelanau County, Michigan, 1931

At the top of the high hill located on 614, a mile and a half from Burdickville, is a view that is a favorite of those who go abroad in the world seeking beauty. Glen Lake puts on a great show at this point — in which the bridge, the Sleeping Bear Sand Dune, Lake Michigan and the Manitou Islands play an important part. There is a very good turnout and parking place on Inspiration Point, and during the summer it is never without a group of summer visitors who have gathered to pay homage to the Goddess of Beauty. Inspiration Point is rightly named. Be sure and include this view in your itinerary. It will be good for your soul. Here you will find a perfect picture of peace.

— "Vacation Handbook and Fisherman's Guide, Leelanau County,"
Leelanau Enterprise, 1940

Glen Lake, from Inspiration Point

Glen Lake in the morning sunshine is a bowl of pure turquoise about five miles long and two and a half miles wide and it is unblemished by any unsightly structures… Those beholding it for the first time do not gush. Instructed by their good example, I here restrain myself. Suffice to repeat, it is the crown jewel of a county whose name — Leelanau — means "delight of life." Those Ojibways could pack a canoe load of poetry into three syllables.

— Bennett, *West Michgan's Flaming Forests*,
West Michigan Tourist Association, 1935

Glen Lake Resorts

There are already six summer resorts on the shores of Glen Lake, and room for a score more. The 20 miles of beach with groves of virgin forest coming almost to the water is a combination rarely found.

Gregory's Resort, which is a little to the south of the village of Glen Arbor, has an eastern exposure. The place is under the management of Mrs. A. W. Gregory, whose post office address is Glen Arbor.

Ray's Resort is near the bridge that crosses the lake at the narrows which divides the waters into two lakes. The place is well managed by W. C. Ray, Glenmere.

Cedar Springs Lodge occupies a commanding spot on the north side of the smaller lake. It is surrounded by beautiful forest. Address S. S. Burke, Glenmere.

Cold Springs Resort, located in the south shore, is in charge of John Biddleman, Empire. The comfort and pleasure of the guests is the constant thought here.

Mrs. H. C. King, Empire, has made Kenwood a popular resort. The place was formerly a farm home, but has been enlarged so as to make comfortable the summer guests.

At the eastern end of Glen Lake is Asher Atkinson's place. This is famous because of the trout stream that runs across the farm. Mr. Atkinson's post office address is Burdickville.

— *Grand Traverse Region*, circa 1914

Cold Spring Resort, Glenmere, Mich.

Kenwood Resort on Glen Lake. Mrs. H. C. King, Empire, Mich.

Cedar Springs Lodge, Glenmere

Hello Gale,
I am having a fine time, lots of resorters here this year. There is going to be an excursion to the island next Sunday, one of the large P.M. boats is coming up here. Suppose that reminds you of cherries. Ha Ha, how about it, are you canning this year? Write soon,

— Eddie

Postmarked Empire, 1909
Mailed to Chicago, Illinois.

Little Indian Brook Trout Pond & Summer Resort

In 1895 J.C. Lardie established a resort at the eastern end of Glen Lake. It was popular with fisherman as it had a trout stream running across the property. The stream is now known as Hatlen's Creek. For many years the resort was known as Asher Atkinson's.

Cold Springs Inn

Cold Springs Inn is situated within a stone's throw of the beautiful Sandy Beach of Glen Lake and at the most sightly point and near the best fishing and boating locality the lake affords. The Inn is modern and convenient. The building contains commodious sitting rooms — dining rooms and large airy bedrooms. The entire building is surrounded by wide porches. Within a few feet of the Inn there are several wonderful Springs of almost ice cold water — great streams pop out of Mother Earth inviting you to partake of its health-giving medicinal qualities — this water is as clear and pure as crystal. You will make many a trip to the Springs and every sip will do you good.

The Inn is managed by experienced resort people that know how, and you feel right at home ten minutes after your arrival. You will be well fed — and they know you have some appetite after a few days in this invigorating climate.

Cold Springs Inn offers a rare combination — a paradise for children and admirable appointed (quarters) for the family outing. The sanitary conditions are excellent. Those who need rest and quiet combined with outdoor life and nourishing food will find Cold Springs Inn with its excellent table and beautiful environs, an ideal place to recuperate.

— Cold Springs Inn on Beautiful Glen Lake, circa 1920

ADVERTISEMENT — OCKER'S INN

— "Vacation Handbook and Fisherman's Guide, Leelanau County," *Leelanau Enterprise,* 1942

Ocker's on Glen Lake

Ockers on Glen Lake.

Ockers Offers Quiet Retreat

Offering a quiet haven to weary travelers, and overlooking the glorious blue waters of Glen Lake, Ocker's Resort, one mile west of the narrows, on the south side of Glen Lake has long been a gathering place for those who want rest and comfort at a reasonable cost.

In conjunction with the regular dining room accommodations for guests, dinners are served on Sundays to visitors from the region, or sight-seers from nearby cities. Home cooked meals are served in Ocker's dining room, and have established a reputation for the resort as an excellent place in which to spend a weekend or a month.

The flowing well, from which all drinking water is taken, is deep and the temperature remains at its same coldness all the year round.

Rooms at Ockers are large and from any window a visitor can see both tree covered hills and sparkling water.

Recreation golf and tennis facilities are nearby and boats are furnished for fishing and riding. Ocker's is close to "Top of the World" undoubtedly one of the most beautiful spots in the United States, and perhaps in the world.

Modern conveniences throughout are for the convenience of discriminating patrons.

— *Traverse City Record Eagle,* June 30, 1937

Ray's Resort, Glen Lake

ADVERTISEMENT — RAY'S RESORT
— *Traverse City Record Eagle, 1938*

Ray's Inn Holds the Promise of Rest and Quiet

Quiet, congenial surroundings, comfortable beds, wholesome meals, and an atmosphere of friendliness make Ray's Inn live up to its motto — "A modern hotel with a home-like atmosphere."

Ray's Inn is located at the Glen Lake Narrows, a few hundred feet north of the bridge, close to activities of every sort. Ray's does not force activity upon its guests. Rather, it seeks to let them rest, or play at will.

The Inn itself and several cottages are arranged along the shore of Glen Lake, and from the windows of the Inn can be secured a view of the hills, the sky, and the ever changing colors of the lake. Large, delightfully pleasant rooms invite one to sleep, and when one is rested the wide screened-in porch, and the cool dining room are other invitations to rest and relaxation.

Food is of the finest, and the management prides itself on the excellent service. Special dinners are prepared, if the guest prefers, and every other means is taken to insure the comfort of each guest.

Swimming in Glen Lake in unexcelled, horses and shuffleboard courts are for the pleasure of the guests, and boating and fishing are available.

Then, when the sports are over, guests gather in large friendly circles, to read, visit, or just rest, with such home-like attractions as fruits, candies of all kinds, and the Inn's specialty, home-made fudge, placed on tables conveniently within reach.

The Inn is under the management of Mrs. Marjorie Jacobs, who personally supervises its operations. Mrs. Jacobs has placed a standing invitation to all vacationists in the region to stop at Ray's Inn, whether they intend to stay or not, just for the visit. The Inn extends its hospitality to all, and all are welcome, at any time.

— *Traverse City Record Eagle, June 30, 1937*

Ray's Resort, Glen Lake, Michigan.

Tonawathya

It is reported that Tonawathya, the resort owned by
Mr. and Mrs. F.A. Gregory is filled to capacity at
this time. Over sixty guests are being cared for, many
living in cottages belonging to the resort. About
eighteen people constitute the personnel for service.

— *Leelanau Enterprise*, August 8, 1940

Carr's Cabin Camps

Accommodations Fine

On Glen Lake Narrows is situated Carr's Cabin Camp, and boat livery. A lack of
boats has always been the greatest difficulty of people anxious to take short trips
around Glen Lake. Mr. Carr has solved this problem with his fleet of fifteen good
boats. The Cabin Camps have a unique feature that makes them popular. Each
sleeping room and housekeeping apartment has an opening off it. This affords the
greatest convenience to tourists who like a protected place to unload their cars.
The cabins have electric lights and running water. There is a store in connection
with the camp.

Mr. Carr has built an absolutely modern apartment house off the shore
of the lake within a short distance of the cabins.

— *Traverse City Record Eagle*, June 29, 1931

A Fine Welcome at MacDonald's

Vacationists visiting this region and wishing to partake of the excellent fishing, swimming and boating that Glen Lake, what some people call "the most beautiful lake in the United States" affords, will find a warm welcome at MacDonald's on M-22 at the Narrows. Standing but a few steps from the water's edge are the living quarters for those making this spot their temporary abode. The several apartments are furnished in a comfortable, homelike manner suitable to sportsmen.

Nothing can quite equal an invigorating early morning dip in the sparkling, blue water of Glen Lake. Then to a breakfast of pancakes, bacon and steaming coffee with an appetite that calls for "more" with every bite. After a period of relaxation in the shade afforded by the surrounding woodland, you will, no doubt, be ready to take a rowboat and go out to pit your skill against that of the countless bass, perch and pickerel which lurk in the lake waters. After a long summer day of pleasant pastime you will indeed be ready to eat a hearty evening meal and retreat to bed.

— Traverse City Record Eagle, June 30, 1935

Juniper Cottage Tea Room

GLEN LAKE, MICHIGAN

Tea rooms were popular in the 1920s and 1930s. Light meals were generally served. This kind of fare was appealing to summer vacationers and motorists who wanted a quick bite.

ADVERTISEMENT — JUNIPER COTTAGE TEA ROOM
— *Leelanau Enterprise*, 1939

Rustic Bridges, Muerer Grounds, Glen Lake, Mich.

Glen Lake, Mich. July 30, 1930

Dear Friends,

It was one month yesterday that we came here.

It has been some month, will tell you about it

when we see you. How we wish you, Clarence

and the children could be here and have a dip with

us. The sunsets are beautiful and there is a lot of

pretty scenery. Times are not very lively this summer.

The weather has been offely hot here, but not as bad

as at home from what we hear. Mr. H. gets drunk

quite often — twice a month and don't things get hot then.

— Love to all, Hazel and Lottie —

Postmark, date, address not shown

Gene's Summer Home

Glen Lake had its share of celebrities. Gene Carroll and Glenn Rowell of "Jake and Lena" radio fame both had summer homes on Glen Lake. Gene's Summer Home is shown to the left and Glenn's is shown below. Their show could be heard in the late 1930s on WLS in Chicago at 7:00 a.m. every day.

Glenn's Summer Home

Little Glenn's Log Cabins

Cabin Village Lovely Place

Numbered among this season's new summer resorts, Little Glenn's Log Cabin Village, situated on the east end of Glen Lake at Burdickville, presents to the summer visitor some of the cleanest, most completely equipped and most ideally located individual cottages on the lake.

The cottages, numbering eight, and the central community kitchen were all built this spring and are constructed of split logs and finely furnished. The cabins are small and cozy with a large screen surface so that they may be kept cool

and airy at all times. All cottages have electric conveniences and comfortable beds. The community kitchen is equipped with running water and shower baths, as well as complete facilities for cooking and preparing meals, including iceboxes. All equipment, bedding, cooking utensils, and so forth are furnished.

By virtue of its advantageous position on the sandy shores of crystal clear Glen Lake, the bathing beach is excellent and safe for children. The boats which may be rented provide many happy hours of rowing on this body of water which has been called one of the most beautiful lakes in the world. Fishing equipment is available either for angling for the Mackinaw trout, which are present in the lake, or for the brook and rainbow trout, which are plentiful in many nearby streams. Only a short drive from the Log Cabin Village, the Glen Lake Course and the Day Forest Estate Course furnish scenic, sporty golfing for those who enjoy this recreation. Horses may be secured upon request for riding purposes.

From Little Glenn's Log Cabin Village may be obtained a gorgeous panoramic view of the sand dunes bordering Lake Michigan, a view which might inspire some of the more adventurous guest to take the thoroughly fascinating and educational hike over these sandy wastelands.

— Traverse City Record Eagle, June 30, 1934

Green Dragon is Very Unique

After two highly successful years, the Green Dragon, presenting an appeal entirely unique to the resorter, and unduplicated throughout the region, has reopened for the summer trade.

True to its name, the bewilling roofs of this unusual structure are ornamented at four peaks with brilliant green, hand carved dragons. The harsh black and orange of the building itself lends an oriental atmosphere which is intriguing. The Green Dragon is an accurate reproduction, both in structure, and in service of a Japanese Tea Garden.

At the road entrance is a fantastically shaped Japanese "Torrie" and a short distance from the building a quaint little Japanese bridge arches over a small stream.

Oriental dishes are served at the Green Dragon, in a like atmosphere. A spotless kitchen and a Chinese cook combine in the preparation of these fine dishes.

The Green Dragon features a summer "Cocktail Hour" every afternoon from four to five. Dancing is enjoyed nightly to the strains of Jimmy Lowe's Commadores, who played at the Blue Boat Inn in Detroit this winter. A complete bar service is available.

The Green Dragon, owned and managed by Mrs. Gene Carroll, former wife of Gene of the radio team of Gene and Glenn, is located on the south side of Glen Lake, one half mile from Burdickville. The management promises its guests a good time.

— Traverse City Record Eagle, June 30, 1935

Advertisement — The Green Dragon, 1934

— Traverse City Record Eagle, 1934

Holden Resort has Wide Fame

On the large Glen Lake, called one of the most beautiful lakes on the world, is to be found a little resort center which, though small in size, is large in fame. Holden's Resort holds its claim to fame chiefly upon its ability to make visitors feel at home, and prepare chicken, steak, and fish dinners that "please the palate."

Holden's Resort is situated in Burdickville, and has a general store in connection. Tourists' cabins as well as tourists' rooms are obtainable. The situation is especially desirable because of its nearness to Sleeping Bear, the famous sand dunes only nine miles away."

— *Traverse City Record Eagle,* June 30, 1933

Holden's Tourist Cabins

MAP OF BURDICKVILLE, *Atlas of Leelanau County*, 1900
Burdickville is located on the southeastern shore of Glen
Lake, 26 miles northwest of Traverse City and nine
miles south of Glen Arbor. In 1900 Burdickville had a
population of 75 inhabitants. It had a sawmill, a saw and
grist mill, a general store and hotel, a blacksmith, two
carpenters, a music teacher, and a justice of the peace.

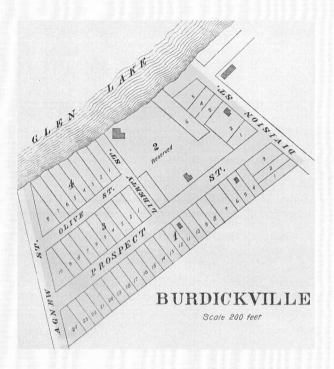

The Holden's store, shown here about
1925, was the center of life in Burdickville
for many years. It was established by John
Helm in 1867, and changed hands several
times until John Holden took over the
operation in 1923.

Camp Davis, Burdickville

Camp Davis — students of the University of Michigan School of Engineering had the opportunity to spend the summers from 1902 to 1908 on Glen Lake at Burdickville. The technical skills the students learned in Ann Arbor were put to field practice in the Glen Lake area.

Engineering students, Camp Davis

Baxters's Standard Service, Burdickville

The Baxter gasoline station is now in operation. Its pleasing appearance with its beautiful lighting system is a great asset to the village and is located on its most prominent corner (M-614 and M-616), where one gets their first view of Glen Lake coming from Traverse City.

— *Leelanau Enterprise*, June 3, 1937

Top of the World — *This scenic and beautiful spot is located about one mile from the village of Burdickville, and you reach it by one half mile of paved road, until you reach the picturesque forks where the paved and wooded country road meet — signs there will direct you to this exquisite view. Roads have been made to the summit of this view hill, from which you look out upon a vista that takes in the far away North and South Manitou Islands and the blue waters of Lake Michigan, and the nearer view of lovely Glen Lake which includes the bridge at the Narrows, a view of the upper lake beyond the bridge and a grand and extended view of the noted sand dune, Sleeping Bear. This is privately owned property, Mr. Oscar Johnson of Grand Rapids being the owner, but the beauties of the Top of the World are accessible to any visitor who chooses to visit the spot. This is a favorite spot for artists who will often be found there endeavoring to transfer to canvas a picture that almost beggars description, as far as words are concerned.*

— "Vacation Handbook and Fisherman's Guide, Leelanau County,"
Leelanau Enterprise, 1940

Scotty's Haven

Dear Don and Edna,
This is where we are and its beautiful as ever. Its quite cool today, it rained both nights so far. They get lots of thunderstorms here. Fishing is good, we have 30 or 40 fish in the ice box now. We've been feeding all the company fish. Hope everything is fine there.

— Adolph, Rose & Steven

Postmarked Glen Arbor, 1949
Mailed to Nashville, Michigan

SCOTTY'S HAVEN   GLEN LAKE, MICH G 2839

Glen Lake Golf Course "Sporty"

The course is laid out compactly on rolling hills. From the club house there is a magnificent view of Glen Lake, Lake Michigan and the Manitou Islands. It is the boast of the club that there is a beautiful view from every tee.

This nine-hole course of twenty-eight hundred and seventy-five yards is sporty and in as good condition as it is possible to keep it. It is an attractive course for the golfer who enjoys a good game.

Besides the course, this one hundred twenty acres has a clubhouse which is the social center of Glen Lake. The good dance floor gets much use throughout the summer. There is a refreshment service during parties.

One of the interesting features of the club is the cement pool, built on a little stream that runs through the land. This is filed [sic] with goldfish. Clubs and equipment are available.

— *Traverse City Record Eagle*, June 29, 1931

Excellent Golf Links Overlook Glen Lake

Eighteen-Hole Course One of the Most Sightly and Sportiest in Michigan.

Looking down on Glen Lake, one of the five most beautiful lakes in the world, with the same view as that secured by the eagle in flight, is the eighteen hole Glen Lake golf course, promoted by the Glen Lake Golf and Country Club.

No more sightly location can be found in the middle west for a golf course than that selected by this club. From nearly every fairway and from the high porch of the club house one may gaze down into the very depths of the beautiful lake.

But the club boasts something beside view. It is one of the sportiest courses in the north and is also one of the very few 18-hole courses to be found in the Michigan resorts. The topography of the course is decidedly rolling and presents hazards which even professionals cannot consistently conquer. More and more the course is being played, not only by golf enthusiasts from the Glen Lake region but from many of the resorts farther away.

The club has a commodious and well planned club house with all the things which go to make the headquarters comfortable and attractive. The club is unique in that it is far away from any city. The nearest place of any considerable size is Traverse City, 27 miles away. It is decidedly unusual to find so excellent a golf course so far from a center of population. But it must be remembered that, while there is no centralized community in the region, all of Glen Lake, Glen Haven, Glen Arbor, and the other settlements in the district thrown together would make a city of considerable size during the summer months.

It is the popularity of Glen Lake as a summer resort among the people of the middle west which made it possible to establish and maintain so pretentious a golf course.

— Traverse City Record Eagle, July 31, 1926

Note: Dreams were bigger than reality. The course is actually a nine-hole course

White Cottage, Glen View

"THE "WHITE COTTAGE" GLEN VIEW   GLEN ARBOR, MICH.   C-2824

Glen View

Deluxe Modern Cottages

Glen View on Glen Lake has a beach of hard sand, clear pure water, safe bathing for youngsters and dock and diving raft are provided. Outboard motors and sailboats are available in the near vicinity at nominal fees.

At Glen View you may enjoy swimming, fishing, climbing Sleeping Bear Sand Dunes or riding over the dunes in a dunemobile, a canoe trip down the Crystal River, bicycling, sailing, water skiing, scuba diving, fishing for Lake Trout, beach parties and horseback riding at Circle "H" Ranch.

Glen View Cottages offer modern city conveniences at Glen Lake — electric refrigerators, modern cooking ranges, hot and cold water, inside plumbing, showers, innerspring mattresses, comfortable furniture, as well as excellent, safe swimming and good fishing. We serve family groups which are looking for a nice quiet place to rest and spend a peaceful vacation.

— *Peppler's on Beautiful Glen Lake, circa 1965*

Advertisement — Glen View

— *Vacation Days in Michigan's Grand Traverse Bay Region,*
Traverse City Area Chamber of Commerce, circa 1958

108

The Pioneer Cabins that are nearing completion are a great
addition to the resort business of Glen Lake. These cabins are
attractively built and occupy an attractive location adjacent to
the Old Settlers picnic grounds. They are built on a ridge or a
slight rise of ground, that gives a wonderful view of Glen Lake.
They are strictly modern in every way, with running water,
electricity, etc. They are cabins where one will not just want
to spend a night, but a week or a month. There are outdoor
tables and stove, and later on a tennis court and shuffleboard
will be added.

— *Leelanau Enterprise*, June 23, 1938

Old Settler's Picnic Grounds

The Old Settlers' picnic grounds located adjacent to the village
of Burdickville, is one of the county's choicest possession. It
comprises 6 acres bordering on Glen Lake and is the only park
located on the lake. It is covered with beautiful trees, there is a
fine spring of water, and comfortable seats and tables for the
convenience of visitors. The park has an interesting history
and was the outgrowth of the Old Settler's picnic that is held
annually, on August 3rd. The date, August 3rd, was chosen
for its being the birthday of one of the earliest pioneers of the
region, Kasson Freeman, after whom Kasson Township was
named. On the day of this picnic sons and daughters of the
early pioneers who have located to the far ends of the United
States journey home by train, car or airplane in order to keep
their touch with the "days that are gone" and to honor the memory of the Old Settlers of Leelanau
County. The grounds are located on 616 near the junction of 614.

— "Vacation Handbook and Fisherman's Guide, Leelanau County,"
Leelanau Enterprise, 1942

Glen View,
Glen Lake

Regatta, Glen Lake

There is to be a regatta on Glen Lake today...and we can see the sailing craft and motor boats assembling near Gregory's where the take-off will take place. It is ideal day, with a stiff breeze and the lake looking as though several bottles of blueing had been dropped into it.

— *Leelanau Enterprise,* July 18, 1942

Regatta, Glen Lake Country Club.

Dunn's Resort

Private Cottages with Central Dining Room.
Transients Welcomed at all times.
P.O. Maple City, R. 1
East Side of Glen Lake County Road 4

Advertisement — *Leelanau Enterprise,* August 5, 1926

Dunn's Farm, Glen Lake

Glen Eden Hotel

Glen Eden for a fine vacation

*Glen Eden is a quiet comfortable place to spend a vacation.
The location is woodsy and the hotel is built in perfect harmony
with the setting. Modern conveniences have been installed
without spoiling the rustic charm of the hotel.*

*Bedrooms are arranged in suites for family use. For
those who wish to be by themselves, there are two sleeping
cottages within a short distance from the main lodge.*

*Glen Lake provides the guests with good swimming and
fishing. Boats are available.*

— Traverse City Record Eagle, June 29, 1931

Glen Eden Hotel, Glen Lake, Mich.

Glen Arbor

Glen Arbor is situated on the shores of Lake Michigan at the mouth of the Crystal River, opposite South Manitou Island. It is located 30 miles northwest of Traverse City, and 30 miles southwest of Northport.

About 1847 John La Rue traveled to South Manitou Island to improve his health. He stayed on the island for a while and traded with the Native Americans. He returned to Chicago but came back the following year and settled on the mainland at the mouth of the Crystal River, where he built a log cabin, becoming the first European permanent settler on the mainland of Leelanau County.

A few years later, in 1854, John Dorsey and John Fisher arrived in the area. Fisher built a log cabin at Glen Arbor and bought 1,000 acres of land on the north side of Glen Lake. He became the first supervisor of the township when it was organized in 1856 as part of what was then Grand Traverse County. It is Fisher's wife who is credited with naming Glen Arbor, inspired by the sylvan beauty of the tall trees surrounding a quiet hollow which was once Native American council grounds.

Soon other pioneers followed; more than two dozen were family and friends of the Fishers. In 1857 a dock and wooding station were built. Cordwood was cut and sold to the passing steamers. In 1859 John Fisher erected a sawmill on the Crystal River. He named the river after the pure, crystal-clear flowing water. The small lake, or outlet, to the north of Glen Lake is named Fisher Lake because his property surrounded it.

Lumbering was an important economic force in the area. In 1899 J.O. Nessen formed the Glen Arbor Lumber Company and erected a large sawmill on the west shore of Glen Lake. Nessen purchased a steam locomotive and

A STREET SCENE IN GLEN ARBOR

Glen Arbor is completely nestled "among the pines" and oaks, which give it a pleasant appearance at all seasons of the year. It has about 200 inhabitants, one wood dock, owned by the Todd brothers, who also have a store; another store by Mr. William H. Cook; blacksmith and cooper shops, etc. This village is situated between the elegant little Glen Lake and Lake Michigan and business men of the town propose to cut a canal to connect the two lakes.

— Traverse Region, Historical and Descriptive, 1884

built a rail line from his mill to the dock at Glen Arbor. He operated successfully for a few years, but in 1907 he dismantled the mill and sold the locomotive to D.H.Day.

Lumbering had not been the only activity in the area. A few families supported themselves by fishing, barrel making, and farming. In 1870 Dr. William Walker discovered that the marshes around Glen Arbor were excellent for cranberry production, and he raised large crops each year. He also planted fruit trees and successfully raised apples and cherries. Other early farmers soon followed, including the Miller family after whom Miller Hill was named. For many years the Glen Arbor docks were busy shipping lumber, fish, and fruit to Chicago.

By 1910 the Glen Lake region was becoming known as an attractive resort area. Resorts were springing up along the Glen Lake shore, and the village of Glen Arbor had an influx of visitors. The Grady Inn, which had served as living quarters for lumberjacks, was converted into a tourist hotel. The name was changed to the Sylvan Inn and by 1920 it was catering exclusively to tourists.

Walkers Inn was located on Lake Michigan near the dock at Glen Arbor. It was more elegant than the other resorts in the area and even had a ballroom. Diners were provided with the finest linens and silverware. The hotel was a favorite stop for salesmen traveling by steamship. Walkers Inn was originally operated by Dr. Walker and his wife Elisa, then later by their daughter Estelle. Her son, George Grady, was operating the Inn in 1914 when it was consumed by fire.

Another early hotel was Langrick's Inn, which had been a boarding house for lumberjacks. In 1916 it was purchased by Carl and Martha Andresen.

Having a rotten time.
Flat tires and engine trouble.
— Randy

Postmarked Glen Arbor, circa 1925
Mailed to Saginaw, Michigan

CRYSTAL RIVER SERVICE STATION GLEN ARBOR MICH

In the 1930s it became a popular Glen Arbor dining spot called the "Kum-an-Dyne." Tourist cabins were added to accommodate overnight guests.

The Homestead near Glen Arbor had its beginnings as Camp Leelanau for Boys, which was founded in 1921 by Cora and William "Skipper" Beals. The camp had a staff of Christian Scientists and accommodated 150 boys, ages six to sixteen. The summer program included swimming, water skiing, canoeing, overnight camping trips, horseback riding, arts and crafts, Indian and nature lore, competitive sports, and many other activities to challenge the interests and abilities of the boys. Gradually, the camp evolved to a year-round enterprise called the Leelanau Schools.

The Beals' old farmhouse was known as "The Homestead," and originally had accommodations for some of the boys. About 1940 girls were admitted to the Pinebrook School. Dormitories for the students were turned into guest rooms for the summer and the Homestead became a guest inn. In 1943 Arthur and Helen Huey purchased the school and operated it as a privately owned institution until 1963, when it was reorganized as a nonprofit foundation. The Homestead Resort became a separate entity from the school and has grown into Glen Arbor's finest resort.

As tourism became more important to the economy of Glen Arbor, more shops and services opened that catered to the tourist trade. The Glen Arbor Gift Shop sold souvenirs from the area and the Sportsman's Shop catered to the many fishermen. Glen Arbor has grown in recent years but still maintains its small-town charms and is a mecca to visitors in the Glen Lake region.

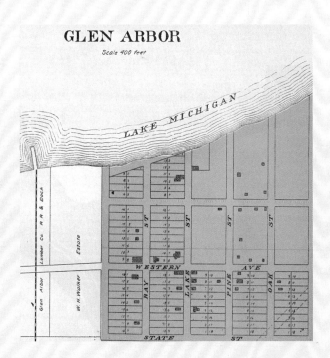

MAP OF GLEN ARBOR *Atlas of Leelanau County,* 1900
Glen Arbor is located on Sleeping Bear Bay, 18 miles southwest of Leland, and 28 miles northwest of Traverse City. In 1900 Glen Arbor had a population of 200. There was a dock and sawmill, a gristmill, five fruit growers, a livery, a hotel, a general store, two coopers, a blacksmith, a cranberry grower, a physician, a poolroom, and a saloon.

"S.S. Missouri" at dock, Glen Arbor

The S. S. *Missouri* of the Northern Michigan Transportation Company at the Glen Arbor dock, circa 1910. The steamship line promoted "attractive weekend trips" for the "busy businessman." One could leave Chicago at 6:00 p.m. on Friday, arrive at Glen Arbor Saturday at 8:45 a.m., enjoy the weekend, and arrive back in Chicago by 8:30 a.m. on Monday.

Glen Arbor, Mich.

Walkers Inn Glen Arbor, Mich.

Walkers Inn was located on Lake Michigan near the dock in Glen Arbor. It was more elegant than the other resorts in the area and even had a ballroom. Diners were provided with the finest linens and silverware. It was a favorite stop for salesmen traveling by steamship. It was originally operated by Dr. Walker and his wife Elisa, then later by their daughter Estelle, Her son George Grady was operating the Inn in 1914 when it was consumed by fire.

Walkers Inn

Walkers Inn Glen Arbor, Mich.

Grady's Inn / The Sylvan Inn

Grady's Inn operated as the Sylvan Inn for much of the twentieth century.
It originally served as quarters for lumberjacks, but with the decline of
lumbering, the Sylvan Inn began to "cater exclusively to tourists."

SYLVAN INN GLEN ARBOR, MICHIGAN
Fine Home Cooking, Country Style. Good Beds. Fine and
airy, on Lake Michigan in the Woods.
CATER EXCLUSIVELY TO TOURISTS   PHONE FOR RESERVATIONS

ADVERTISEMENT — SYLVAN INN
— *King's Official Route Guide,* 1920

Oak Dale, Glen Arbor

Hello Everyone: We are at Glen Lake, Michigan and having a wonderful time. Caught 40 fish today, some fish-fry! Ramble roses are blooming, cherries are ripe & the fields are green. We climbed sand dunes today. Wish you could see this place.

— Love, Hudson

Postmarked Empire, 1946
Mailed to Findlay, Ohio

Glen Arbor Gift Shop

The Glen Arbor Gift Shop was opened in 1938 by Robert Oleson and Jack Rader, who bought out his partner the following year. The original building was moved in 1947 and a new and larger shop was erected on the site. That same year Jack Rader married Mary Foster and together they operated the store as "Rader's" until 1972 when the business was sold to new owners. Now called the "Totem Gift Shop," it remains a popular attraction in Glen Arbor.

ADVERTISEMENT — KUM-AN-DYNE

—"Vacation Handbook and Fisherman's Guide," Leelanau County,

Leelanau Enterprise, 1938

The Redwood
Overnight Cabins
In Connection

Horse Shoe Court
Croquet, Ping Pong
Grove Wired for Trailers

Kum-An-Dyne

Mrs. Andresen's

●

Delicious Chicken Dinners

Steak   Fish

●

Glen Arbor — Michigan

On M—22

Kum-an-Dyne has Good Food

Kum-an-Dyne, possibly you have seen this sign in the course of your travels in Leelanau County. At Glen Arbor the Kum-an-Dyne, Mrs. Andresen proprietor, is recognized as a good place to eat. In good weather guests eat out on a shady screened-in porch, or they may have private dining quarters.

Four overnight cabins have been built of redwood to accommodate the demand for sleeping quarters. Each of the cabins is equipped with electricity and running water. Back sections of each cabin can be removed to allow an excellent view of Lake Michigan. The spot is only a short distance from the lake and just a short drive from Glen Lake. It can be classed as a focal point for all of the activities surrounding this district, including boating, bathing, horseback riding, golfing, aeroplaning, fishing and a hundred and one other forms of diversion.

— *Traverse City Record Eagle*, June 30, 1935

Sportsman Shop

Glen Arbor — *Heart of the old lumbering operations.*
Glen Arbor is one of the centers of Glen Lake activity.
Scenically situated under towering pines between Lake
Michigan and Glen Lake. Glen Arbor is one of the most
beautiful villages in Leelanau County.

— *M-22 "The Manitou Trail,"* 1955

Steffens Grocery

This is certainly a wonderful
place to rest.— and I lost my
"bark" somewhere — am not
looking for it either.

— Cookie

Postmarked Glen Arbor, circa 1940
Mailed to Battle Creek

Bourne's Restaurant, Glen Arbor

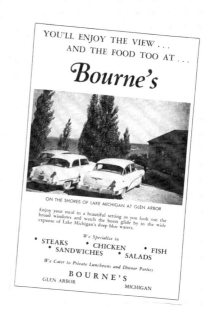

YOU'LL ENJOY THE VIEW...
AND THE FOOD TOO AT...

Bourne's

ON THE SHORES OF LAKE MICHIGAN AT GLEN ARBOR

Enjoy your meal in a beautiful setting as you look out the broad windows and watch the boats glide by in the wide expanse of Lake Michigan's deep blue waters.

We Specialize in
• STEAKS • CHICKEN • FISH
• SANDWICHES • SALADS

We Cater to Private Luncheons and Dinner Parties

BOURNE'S
GLEN ARBOR   MICHIGAN

ADVERTISEMENT — BOURNE'S
— Vacation Days in Michigan's Grand Traverse Region,
Traverse City Chamber of Commerce, 1955

La-Moderene Cottage   H 22
Glen Arbor
Michigan

Hi Folks,
Everything swell and in the pink
of condition. No worry in the world.
— "Marv"

Postmarked Maple City, circa 1950
Mailed to North Muskegon, Michigan

Crystal River

In traveling throughout the country, one begins by being amused but ends by being slightly annoyed at the names given on road maps and signboards describing places of interest lying ahead. Names that on first reading intrigue you, causing you to speed up and raising your expectations high, only to dash them to the ground when you arrive upon the actual scene.

But Crystal River of Leelanau County is different. This river does not intrigue a person's interest only to let them down, for this river is all that its name implies and even more.

It is such an enchanting, friendly river "meandering its cheerful way through green velvety banks" that like the Lorelei of the Rhine, it will lure you from your car to its side. You will not be satisfied with just the mere cursory glance of the ordinary sightseer — indeed, you will not be satisfied at all until you kneel down so that you may gaze into its clear limpid waters.

This river is one of the most interesting and, no doubt, one of the most charming streams in the United States. Geologists have delighted in its meandering and have devoted pages to it in magazine articles. It has its beginning in the Fisher Lake, that charming "little sister" of beautiful Glen Lake, and it loses itself in the blue waters of grand old Lake Michigan.

The tract of land which lies between Fisher Lake and Lake Michigan is just a mile in width, but so devious are the ways of this stream as it goes merrily on its way to the great lake, that its journey covers a distance of nine miles. Like some beauteous maiden it is capricious and changeable in its disposition. It will make a direct and decided turn toward the North only to think better of it and then turn decidedly toward the South. It makes these ox bow turns over and over again, as though reluctant to continue its journey to the "big water" — but at long last it does continue on its way, surrendering itself passionately in a mad swirl of rapid waters as it enters Lake Michigan.

Crystal River, Glen Arbor, Mich.

There is some fine fishing to be had in this wandering gypsy of all rivers, if you are a fisherman. If you are a botanist, on its banks is interesting plant life awaiting your classification. If you are simply one of those in quest of beauty at her loveliest, you will find it here by the side of this, Nature's beautiful child, Crystal River.

There are people who make a pilgrimage every Autumn just to view the gorgeous coloring of the leaves, reflected and truly reproduced in this exquisite mirror. So clear and perfect is this reflection that the very veining of the leaves will be shown with a pencil like sharpness far below the surface of the water.

A Crystal River, thou art, indeed, and rightly named.

— "Vacation Handbook and Fisherman's Guide, Leelanau County,"
Leelanau Enterprise, 1940

Canoers on Crystal River

You resorters, who have been coming to Leland, Northport, Omena and other points for years, probably do not know that there is such a stream as the Crystal River or that there is such a soul satisfying trip as this one…This is such an unspoiled beauty spot. When you are drifting down this stream you feel as though civilization with its myriad worries and cares is far removed — that this is the real world and that the other is just some fretful dream.

— *Leelanau Enterprise,* August 15, 1940

Camp Leelanau for Boys

Camp Leelanau for Boys was founded in 1921 by Skipper and Cora Beals. Camp activities included swimming, sailing, canoeing, outboard motoring, archery, riding, riflery, hiking, overnight camping and several sports. Nature lore and Indian crafts were taught.

Winter vacations were promoted by the Leelanau
Schools. Skiing, snowshoeing, and tobogganing were
among the winter activities enjoyed by the guests.

Enjoy a REAL WINTERY HOLIDAY SEASON IN THE NORTH WOODS!
The HOMESTEAD LEELANAU for BOYS · GLEN ARBOR, MICHIGAN IS OPEN FOR GUESTS
$3.00 a DAY $15.00 per WEEK   SPECIAL RATES for FAMILIES   WRITE FOR INFORMATION

Winter and Summer Fun

ADVERTISEMENT — THE HOMESTEAD

— *Carefree Days in West Michigan,* West Michigan Tourist Association, 1951

Cabins at the Homestead

The Leelanau Homestead

One of America's outstanding family resorts, in scenic surroundings, where the north woods meets the turquoise blue of Sleeping Bear Bay.

The Inn, modern guest cottages, play area, white sand beaches, woodland trails, trout streams, on more than 300 acres of grounds — "like a country estate of your own…"

Fun and games or peace and quiet…that's the way at the Leelanau Homestead. Swim, play tennis or shuffleboard, ride horseback, take part in planned social activities if you wish. Or feel free to rest undisturbed or explore "on your own" the byways around Sleeping Bear Bay.

Guests rave about our delicious, home-cooked meals skillfully served in the new "picture window" terrace dining room overlooking Lake Michigan. In individual pine-paneled cottages, under towering pines, you'll find beds so-o-o-o comfortable you should "sleep like a bear."

Children are welcomed at the Homestead. Sitters are available for those times when parents might choose to go a "jaunt" of their own.

Beach picnics, "float" trips down the Platte River, climbing the incomparable Sleeping Bear Sand Dunes, trips to nearby points of interest — all these are included in summer fun at the Homestead.

— *Leelanau Homestead,* circa 1957

Lake Leelanau Region

Lake Leelanau is a large body of water which lies in one of the north-south valleys created by the retreat of glaciers some 10,000 years ago. It is 16 miles in length and varies in width from a few rods to three miles. The entire shore is indented with bays into which empty some fine trout streams.

Lake Leelanau was formerly known as Carp Lake and the village of Lake Leelanau was called Provemont until about 1924. The name change caused some confusion in the ensuing years, since the railroad still used the name Provemont on its depot and timetables.

The dam built at Leland about 1853 had a drastic impact on Carp Lake. Before the dam was built, there were three different bodies of water beyond the Carp River. The dam raised the water level 12 feet and created one large lake. The narrowest portion of the lake that separated the northern and southern sections was called "The Narrows," and became the site of the village of Provemont.

The name "Provemont," possibly a derivation of the word "improvement," was given to the village by its early settlers about 1860. Provemont had its beginnings when the Schaub family came in 1855 and took up farming. They are credited with planting the first vineyard in Leelanau County. Many of the early settlers were French-Canadians. Other ethnic groups included Germans, Irish, Dutch, and Bohemians. These early settlers built the first wooden bridge across the Narrows in 1864. That early structure was replaced with an iron bridge in 1895, then a concrete bridge in 1939.

The first mill, a combined grist and sawmill, was built in 1884 on the east side of the Narrows. *The Traverse City Evening Record* wrote in 1906:

> *"Provemont may justly be styled one of the biggest little towns in Leelanau County. Surrounded by hundreds of acres of fertile land, and fortunately having a milling concern that employs in the neighborhood of sixty men, the year round, it gives it an activity that is remarkable."* [1]

By 1906 Provemont had a population of about 200. Besides the sawmill, it had a feed mill, a shingle mill, two general stores, a hardware store, two shoe stores, a meat market, a blacksmith, a barbershop, a livery business, a hotel, and a summer resort.

[1] "Provemont," *The Traverse City Evening Record*, November 20, 1902, page 2.

The success of the village in some part was due to the railroad, which came to Provemont in 1903. It was the railhead for the Lake Leelanau region for the Manistee and Northeastern Railroad. Daily trains ran between Provemont and Traverse City. Provemont was the closest rail connection to Leland, which never had rail service. Connections could be made at Provemont with the steamers that ran up Lake Leelanau to Leland. The lake was a natural highway through the center of the county and the steamer excursions proved a popular route for the many tourists who were coming into the area.

Another settlement in the Lake Leelanau area was Fouch. The earliest settler in Fouch was an African American named Smith, who built a small dock on Carp Lake. Settlers to the north would travel by water to Smith's Landing and then continue overland to Traverse City, eight miles away. In 1866 John R. Fouch bought land in the area, and when the Manistee and Northeastern came through in 1892, it named the station after Fouch. The village received rail service about 10 years earlier than Provemont, so for a time, it was the rail destination of many Leelanau travelers. The small steamers operating out of Fouch were the *Sally*, the *Tiger*, and the *Leelanau*.

Mr. Fouch built a small hotel in 1905 which served as headquarters for fishermen who came to Lake Leelanau for its excellent fishing. The hotel burned down in 1915 and was not replaced. In 1927 the resort business resumed when Daniel Perrin bought Fouch's property and started a summer resort called Perrin's Landing.

By about 1900, the Lake Leelanau region had become well known as a summer resort. This was due in large part to Fountain Point Resort. The artesian well for which it was named was the result of an attempt to drill for oil. In 1867 Mr. A. de Belloy, a native of Paris, France, was looking for oil when he drilled 900 feet and struck a stream of mineral water which has been flowing ever since. L.C. Morrison bought the property some 20 years later and built a small hotel in 1889. Fountain Point was a success. It was soon enlarged to offer 40 guest rooms, a dining room, a social hall, and 24 cottages. It still operates today with much old-fashioned charm.

By the 1920s the Lake Leelanau shore was dotted with resorts and summer homes. The lake was widely known for its excellent fishing. Its waters sported virtually every fish known to the waters of Northern Michigan — Mackinaw trout, black, green and speckled bass, whitefish, pickerel, muskellunge, perch, walleyed pike, sunfish, perch, and speckled trout.

Swimmers — Fountain Point Resort, circa 1910

As more vacationers traveled north in their automobiles, cabin camps and rental cottages grew in popularity. Among those in the Lake Leelanau region were O.J. Plamondon's, Giegler's Landing at Glockamora, Kool-Kove Cottages, Au-She-Gun Landing, Bellevue Cabins, Perrin's Landing, Anchor Cottages, Bil-Lu-Bird, Cedar Haven, Leelanau's Rustic Resort, and the Jolli-Lodge on Lake Michigan. Only a few vacation rentals remain today. The Lake Leelanau region is now home to many private, beautiful summer homes and cottages.

Leland District is Ideal Resort

Kissed by the constant cooling breath of Lake Michigan, backed up by the long scenic stretches of Lake Leelanau, the longest lake in the north, the Leland resort district rests between the two bodies of water like the spirit which exists between mother and child.

Away from the marts of trade, undisturbed by the jangling and tooting of railroads, blessed by the cooling winds and sheltered from summer sun, Leland has but one mission in life — rest.

The Leland resort district is not confined to Leland alone, but spreads up and down Lake Michigan and Lake Leelanau, taking in a dozen or more resort colonies and forming an ideal location for summer people. No place in Michigan has been more lavishly endowed with water and shade than this section, and its very isolation guarantees those lazy summer days which the tired city family craves.

The village of Lake Leelanau, formerly Provemont, is the rail head for the Lake Leelanau district. It is just far enough from the various resorts so that the commercial atmosphere is dissipated by distance.

Leland itself is a prosperous, picturesque settlement, perched on the edge of Lake Michigan with Lake Leelanau a few steps distant on the east. The village is self supporting, boasting such stores as the Leland Mercantile Co., where all of the creature wants of the summer guests can be cared for. It is well fortified with hotels and eating places and is the center of the most pretentious cottage colony in the north.

Scenically Lake Leelanau stands alone among summer places. Mile after mile of lakeshore opens before the eyes of the tourist, each turn in the road and every twist in the shore line opening up a new and more startling vista. A boat trip the length of the twenty mile lake is a treat which few people forget.

— *Traverse City Record Eagle,* July 31, 1926

CANOEING ON LAKE LEELANAU, LELAND, MICH.

Street Scene. Provemont, Mich.

Provemont — *Provemont is a town located at the narrowest point of Carp Lake. It is reached by boat from Fouch or by stage from Sutton's Bay. It is an interesting village, and has a small hotel, of which Mr. Noel Couturier is the proprietor. There is excellent fishing in Carp Lake near this resort.*

— Michigan in Summer, 1904

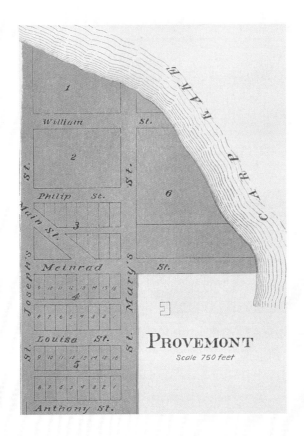

PROVEMONT
Scale 750 feet

MAP OF PROVEMONT *Atlas of Leelanau County,* 1900
Provemont (later to be called Lake Leelanau) is located at the narrows of Carp Lake (later Lake Leelanau), five miles southeast of Leland. It had a sawmill and feed mill, a shingle mill, a general store, two carpenters, a blacksmith, a restaurant and pool hall, a dairy, a Dominican convent, and a popular summer resort.

Manistee and Northeastern RR depot at Provemont, Mich

Provemont

Here there is a post office, a hotel, the Provemont House, a number of stores and other evidences of a thriving country village. It is the terminus of the Leelanau extension on the M. & N. E. R. R. and in daily touch by rail with Traverse City. It is also the nearest railroad point to Leland, which is reached by launch or steamer. The Provemont House, a commercial hotel, is equipped to give good service to anglers and others, with information as to the fishing points, boats, etc.

— *Grand Traverse, the Summer Land,* 1910

Hotel Hahnenberg

Frank Hahnenberg, Prop.,
Provemont, Michigan

This house has just been built and
is opened up to the traveling public.
All new furniture throughout.
It is located so that it commands a
very fine view and in the midst of the
finest Black Bass fishing in
Northern Michigan.
I also have a good feed barn
in connection.

Rates $1.00 per day.
Special rates by the week.
Call and see me and you will
be used right.

The Hotel North was built by Frank Hahnenberg in 1903.

Steamer Leelanau

The steamer *Leelanau* made several stops on Lake Leelanau as it traversed from Fouch to Leland. Among the stops was Fountain Point, a well-known resort that attracted people from all over the Midwest. Fouch was the nearest railroad point for connecting trains from Traverse City.

*The steamer **Leelanau** was detained quite a few moments Friday morning waiting for Wilbur Grobben to bid his lady friend farewell.*

— *Leelanau Enterprise,* August 18, 1904

1 - The Mill and Steamer Leelanau at Provemont, Mich.

Lake Leelanau, Mich.

Lake Leelanau has
Remnant of Early French

Picturesque Lake Leelanau enjoys the novelty of being the only sizeable village within the limits of Leelanau County which is not located on the shore of Lake Michigan.

Located at the Narrows of Lake Leelanau, approximately half way up the lake, the village of Lake Leelanau owes its settlement to the fact that it was a natural gathering place of travelers forced to cross Lake Leelanau in trips from Leland to Suttons Bay, on the opposite side of the Leelanau peninsula.

At one time there was only a rowboat ferry, then a larger ferry, and finally the present bridge.

The village was settled by Frenchmen who in the early days of the region came to the country from Canada and planted a vineyard, now almost entirely gone. The subsequent development of the village, called Provemont in earlier days, and still so named in all railroad guides, was made by another Frenchmen, and today the influence of those early Frenchmen is quite evident on this village.

Here may be seen stores with pure French names prominently displayed. Here may be seen a Catholic Church, convent and school, around which the entire village is centered...

The French language is still spoken, with excited speakers often breaking into the native tongue, as a faster way of expression. Most children in this town are brought up speaking English and French naturally.

Excellent fishing in Lake Leelanau draws many sportsmen to the village of Provemont, on Lake Leelanau. A good resort hotel, within a mile of Lake Leelanau offers comfortable accommodations for all visitors. And reaching out into the county on all sides are excellent roads, over hills and through valleys, where one may see the county from the inside as well as from the Border.

—Traverse City Record Eagle, June 30, 1937

Fountain Point Resort on Lake Leelanau

Fountain Point is a delightful summer resort on the shores of Lake Leelanau a mile to the south of Provemont. The place gets its name from a mineral spring that summer and winter throws a stream twenty feet into the air. The water, which fills a six inch pipe, comes from a depth of nine hundred feet and has great medicinal value. Its use is invaluable for kidney and stomach trouble and dyspepsia. An analysis of the water reveals among the compounds, magnesia, alumnia and lime sulphates, sodium chloride, silca carbonate, iron hydroxide, sulphuretted hydrogen and carbonic acid gas.

Fountain Point Resort, located on the east shore of the lake, is three hundred feet from the water and thirty feet above it. It is one of the most accessible and attractive places in northern Michigan. The hotel was established in 1889, since which year it has been gaining in popularity. From its spacious porches charming views are to be had. The eye can follow the water southward for five miles and northward to the Provemont bridge. The sleeping rooms are large, airy and well furnished. The guests are assured of an abundance of air and light; also cool restful nights. The table is supplied with vegetables in season from the "Point" farm and farms adjoining. White fish and Mackinaw trout from the Leland fisheries are served, as well as brook trout from nearby streams. A special feature is made in serving all fish caught by guests.

There are twelve cottages near the hotel and these can be rented on reasonable terms. The resort is reached by M. & N. E. R. R. to Fouch or Provemont then by steamer to the "Point" dock.

— Grand Traverse Region, circa 1914

Fountain Point is one of the most easily reached and attractive resorts in Northern Michigan. It was established in 1889 and the liberal patronage justifies the extensive improvements made each year. The house has a frontage of one hundred and eight feet on the west or lake side and sixty feet on the north side. A wide porch extends the full length of the two sides mentioned. Spacious lawn in foreground. Well furnished large airy rooms, electric lighted throughout, large halls, public bath room, fire escapes, large dining room overlooking lake, separate rooms for maids and chauffeurs. Post office and telephone in house, telegraph, express office and physicians handy. The Ashley System of sewage disposal. The Michigan State Board of Health has given this resort its highest approval for cleanliness and sanitary surroundings.

— Fountain Point House and Cottages, 1927

Fountain Point, Lake Leelanau

Amusements — *The large living room with its huge fireplace and cozy corners gives cheer for restful hours with a book or needlework. Evening entertainments — card parties, amateur theatricals, concerts, dancing, victrola, lively dance records up to the minute, and piano. One dance with five piece orchestra a week. Men's lounge with fireplace, pocket and charom billards, table games and the social pipe, cigars, tobacco and candy on sale. Out of doors, walks through clean woods free from animals or reptiles, tennis, excellent cement court, lawn bowls, croquet, quoits, horseshoes, baseball and all other summer amusements. Children are not allowed the privileges of the house at all times. Tournaments in all games and sports for prizes.*

Swimming — *High dive, spring board, take off and float, good sport for young and old. Clean sandy beach for kiddies to paddle and splash about.*

— Fountain Point House and Cottages, 1927

Fountain Point, Lake Leelanau, Mich.

CAUGHT IN LAKE LEELANAU LELAND MICH

Fishing — *Fifty one miles of shoreline and every mile presenting spot after spot where big bass, long pike and small pan fish make their home, is what Lake Leelanau holds for the fisherman. Perhaps no other lake in Michigan has yielded the number of fish that have come out of that excellent water.*

It makes little difference where the fisherman starts to work. It may be off Fountain Point, that pretty resort with its ever flowing fountain, or it may be off the docks at Leland or farther down toward Fouch, the fish are there and in numbers.

Up at the north end of the lake is the home of the Mackinaw trout, and Lake Leelanau was one of the first inland lakes to produce these immense fish. Trolling for them is one of the real fishing joys of summer, and few fishermen neglect this form of sport. All up and down the lake are beds of smaller fish, perch, bluegills and sun-fish who contribute their share to the general sportiness of Lake Leelanau.

Flowing into the lake are a dozen or more trout streams where the speckled trout lie hidden under logs and in the deep pools. This, with the lake fishing, combines to give the sportsman a variety from which he can make his choice secure in the knowledge that he will not be disappointed.

— *Traverse City Record Eagle,* July 31, 1926

Au-She-Gun Landing
Lake Leelanau
R3 Traverse City, Mich.

Hi peoples.

We are in a nice 3 bedroom knotty pine cabin. Fishing is swell. John got a large Bass last night and big blue gills. We could live on fish. Children are wonderful. Tomorrow we are traveling for a day to take in the sites. John Jr. caught two fish and caused quite a panic in the boat. Elaine is OK. We are all happy.

— Dorothy and John

Postmarked Cedar, circa 1953
Mailed to Grand Rapids, Mich.

Au-She-Gun Landing

ADVERTISEMENT — AU-SHE-GUN LANDING

— *Vacation Days in the Grand Traverse Bay Region of Michigan,*
Traverse City Area Chamber of Commerce, circa 1956

Perrins Landing
Lake Leelanau
Traverse City, Mich.

Dan Perrin is Personal Pal of Fisherman

Fishermen resorters, who have been coming to this region for many summers drive straight through, not stopping until they reach the Lake Leelanau resort of their personal friend, Dan Perrin.

Perrin's Landing, at the south end of twenty-one mile long Lake Leelanau, is well situated to catch the lake breezes, and far enough into the woods to provide shade for the lodge and cabins, at all times.

First interest of summer visitors at Perrin's is the fishing from Lake Leelanau, unexcelled anywhere.

A long line of rowboats is anchored off the shore each evening at Perrin's, but in the morning that line dwindles, as party after party departs to fish for an hour, half a day, or the entire day. Two guides are ready at any time to guide fishermen to the best spots for perch, bass, pike, or muskellunge. In the busiest season Dan Perrin, himself, helps in guiding, and no fisherman comes home empty handed, after a day on the lake.

— *Traverse City Record Eagle,* June 30, 1937

ADVERTISEMENT — PERRIN'S LANDING

— *Vacation Days in Michigan's Grand Traverse Region,*
Traverse City Area Chamber of Commerce, 1961

Leland

Leland is located on the west shore of the Leelanau peninsula just opposite North Manitou Island, at the mouth of the Carp River (now Leland River). Leland is 11 miles southwest of Northport and 25 miles northwest of Traverse City.

Leland is the site of one of the oldest and largest Native American settlements in Leelanau County. Not far from the Leland River was the Ottawa village of Mishi-me-go-bing, meaning "the place where the Indian canoes run up the river because there is no harbor." The early settlers called it Leland, it is generally assumed, because of its location on the eastern shore of Lake Michigan, where it received the prevailing westerly winds, so it was the "lee land."

The first European settlers, Antoine Manseau and his family and John H. Miller, arrived from North Manitou Island in 1853. They built a dam at the Carp River and soon afterward a water-powered sawmill. Before the dam was built, there were three different bodies of water beyond the river. The dam raised the water level 12 feet and created one large lake, now called Lake Leelanau, which was navigable all the way to the village of Cedar.

Docks were built in Lake Michigan and a wooding station was established to serve the many steamers en route to Chicago or the Straits. The village grew and by 1867 boasted a population of 200. There were three docks, three general stores, a sawmill, a barrel-stave factory, a hotel, a shoe shop, and a blacksmith shop. In 1870 the Leland-Lake Superior Iron Company built a blast furnace on the north side of the dam, which supplied it with water power. The Iron Company brought iron ore by barge from the Upper Peninsula. It employed as many as 150 men, among these were Native Americans who unloaded the barges. Expansion of the village was rapid at this time, although living conditions were somewhat unpleasant because of the smoke from the company furnace.

At the prompting of the Iron Company, the county seat was moved from Northport to Leland in 1883. Following the action, the *Leelanau Enterprise* also moved to Leland from Northport. Unfortunately, by the next year the iron furnace had become unprofitable. It was sold to a local man who founded the Leland Lumber Company, which operated successful lumbering concerns for several years. By 1900 lumbering in the Leland area was essentially finished.

About this same time, Leland's location and climate were promoted as an ideal vacationland. Omena and Northport were already established as summer resort areas. Vacationers were coming north from

the hot cities of the south. Those summer visitors heading to Leland would come to Traverse City by train, then connect with the Manistee and Northeastern train to Fouch, and later to Provemont. They would then board one of the small steamers that traversed Lake Leelanau from Fouch to Leland. Other summer visitors would take the passenger steamers from Chicago and other Great Lakes ports directly to the Leland dock. Leland never had rail service.

As a result of the influx of summer people, the village began to take on a new life. Although there had been earlier hotels in operation, such as the Leelanau Hotel, more accommodations for visitors were needed. In 1901 Jacob Schwartz built a three-story hotel, the Riverside Inn, on the shore of the river. This hotel burned down in 1924. In the following year, Schwartz converted a building intended for a boathouse into a smaller two-story hotel, which bore the same name.

The Nicholas Hotel was built in 1909. It was a two-story frame building situated on the hill to the east of the village center where it commanded a fine view of both Lake Michigan and Carp Lake (now Lake Leelanau). This structure was destroyed by fire in 1926, but rebuilt the following year and named the New Nicholas. The New Nicholas was a luxury hotel with spacious rooms, each with its own bath and hot and cold running water. The large dining room could seat 250 people. Frequently the dining room would serve as a ballroom for dances. In 1946 it became the Leland Lodge.

The Swiss Inn was built in 1910 in a Swiss style with a low slanted roof and several gables. It had 15 sleeping rooms and a large dining room. Guest cottages were added and it later became the Leelanau Lodge. Other early resorts included the Birchcroft and Round Top.

The appeal of the region brought more and more summer resorters who built cottages on both Lake Michigan and Lake Leelanau. A nine-hole golf course was built about 1918. Sailing and motor boating grew in popularity with the summer residents and the Leland Yacht Club was organized in 1936.

Today the quaint village draws visitors to its shops, galleries, and restaurants. It has become a gathering place for art lovers and a center for cultural activities. For years the fishing settlement along the Leland River has been known as "Fishtown" and has been a popular attraction for tourists and a favorite spot for photographers. Like the visitors of years past, Leland draws today's tourists to its picturesque charms.

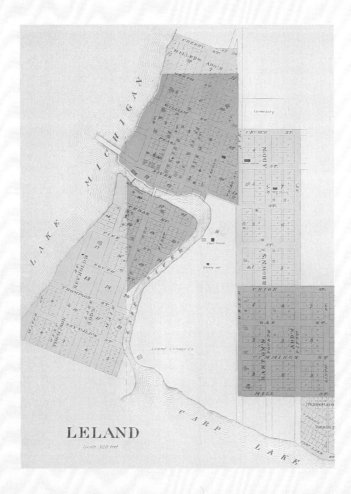

MAP OF LELAND, *Atlas of Leelanau County*, 1900
Leland is located at the mouth of the Carp River, the outlet of Carp Lake (later called Lake Leelanau). Leland lies directly opposite North Manitou Island and is 25 miles northwest of Traverse City. In 1900 the village of Leland had a population of 400. Leland has been the county seat since 1883. It had daily stage service, a weekly newspaper, and Congregational and Lutheran churches. Leland was a shipping point for hardwood lumber, shingles, railroad ties, pig iron, and fish. There was a general store, a hotel, two carpenters, a mason, a shoemaker, a blacksmith, a fisherman, a sheriff, a prosecuting attorney, and a judge.

How to get to Leland

Tourists from Chicago or points on Lake Michigan will find the Peoples Transportation Co. Line very advantageous. Take same to Manistee. There you will connect with the Manistee and North-Eastern Rail Road for Fouch, where you will find the little steamer Leelanau which will take you sixteen miles down Lake Leelanau to Leland. Or passengers may take the Pere Marquette Rail Road to Traverse City, and there get the Manistee and North-Eastern to Fouch (seven miles). Passengers from Toledo and the East may take either the Pere Marquette to Traverse City or may take the Toledo and Ann Arbor to Copemish, and there connect with Manistee and North-Eastern to Fouch.

— *Leland as a Summer Resort,* circa 1903

At the Dock, Leland

The steamship *Missouri* at the dock at Leland about 1910. The *Missouri* was in service from 1904 to 1917. At 2,500 tons she was 225' long by 40' wide and had accommodations for 250 passengers. First-class fare for a round-trip ticket between Chicago and Leland for the "Tourist Season" of 1911 was $11.00. Stateroom and berth fares were extra, ranging from $1.50 to $2.00. Meals on the *Missouri* were served a la carte. Steamships were instrumental in the development of tourism in Leelanau County. Each year they brought thousands of vacationers to the county's summer resorts.

Beautiful Leland!

Like a beautiful gem set forth in a cluster, Leland lies placidly upon the water of Lake Michigan, attracting the traveler and offering every inducement to the tourist to pause for a few days or weeks, to drink in the perfect air and absorb the sunshine that is warranted to be life giving at this quiet place.

Here at this sequestered town — where the waves break wild or gently — either storming or caressing the sands, one can change his mind from "strenuousness" to love.

What calm happiness to stroll through the quiet old town; to drowsily watch the business men do business, or nod your head to a new resorter!

It is doubtful whether there is any other town in America about which so few mosquitoes cling. For many years Leland was the home of an iron furnace, but now we are working up a summer resort trade.

…Leland is quiet and beautiful — all blend into one family, and each person knows the others' affairs like brothers and sisters.

But the town. When the low sun sinks in a bank of clouds the carnelian dyes of the North Manitou Island in royal purple, against which Leland stands out like an entranced village. At times the gold of the sky and the blue of the lake spread out like broad bands — that wave across Leland's front — and look like ribbons woven in the sky…It can get the spirit rejuvenated and the stomach well-filled without much effort of the purse strings.

Then let go into Apostrophe, and sing unto Leland: —

MY LELAND

(Air-America)

My Leland, 'tis of thee
Sweet town of chastity,
   Of thee I sing!
Town where resorters come;
Town to the manor born;
   From every state outside
   Let's crown her queen

     My native village! thee
     Town by the inland sea,
       Thy name I love.
     I love thy lakes and creek,
     Thy streets and houses, me
       My heart with rapture speaks
       Like that above.

Let music swell the breeze,
And ring from all the trees
   Dear Leland's song!
Let local men awake,
Let all that do quake —
Let strangers help to make —
   The town a throng!

— *Leelanau Enterprise*, January 31, 1907

Leland is a comfortable resort. Its hotels offer ease and quiet and good food, and its tea rooms and restaurants set excellent tables at fair prices. The stores in the village are well stocked. There is one, the Leland Mercantile, which years ago had painted on it the legend "Everything from a needle to a steamship," and which still carries on the tradition.

— *Leelanau Enterprise*, July 27, 1932

Hotel Leelanau

— R. Ruff, Proprietor —

Leland, Michigan

This Hotel has been recently supplied with
NEW AND NEAT FURNITURE,
And is now prepared to accommodate
Summer visitors, as well as the
traveling public generally.
The FRESH AIR AND PURE WATER
of Carp Lake and Lake Michigan make the
CLIMATE HERE UNEQUALLED.

Part of Morning's Catch

The hamlet (of Leland) has a permanent population of about 400. It is also the county seat of Leelanau County and here are located many county buildings, and here the court sits and dispenses justice between man and man. The principal industry is that of deep lake fishing. There are a half-dozen or more fishing crews who with their boats, nets, bouys, reels and shanties give a picturesque coloring to the place. These men are real sailors, and daylight each morning, in fishing weather, find them far out on the "great" lake.

— *Grand Traverse Region, circa 1914*

Part of a morning's catch. Leland, Mich.

Leland, Mich.

7-12-19
We are here alright.
This is a picture of
the boat that brought
us over from Fouch.
The pilot is dandy
fellow — he answered
all the foolish questions
we could think of.
                    — J.S.B.

Postmarked Leland, 1919
Mailed to Fort Wayne, Indiana

Lake View Farm

Some farmers opened their homes to visitors when the tourist industry in Leelanau County was still new. A farm vacation was promoted as a wholesome escape from city life. Lake View Farm outside Leland had accommodations for 25 guests at low rates.

Hunter Souvenir Shop, Leland

Few places can hold out such wonderful advantages for comfort and pleasure as Leland…Leland has good supply stores from which all of the necessities can be procured at a very reasonable charge. In fact our summer friends all speak highly of the treatment accorded to them by Leland Citizens.

— *Leland as a Summer Resort,* circa 1903

Old Riverside Inn

The Riverside Inn, under the management of Mr. Schwartz, houses a happy throng every season. The house is large and comfortable with fifty fine, airy rooms. It is open the year around, and gives one the solid permanent, homelike comfort that many exclusively summer homes lack. The guests enjoy a bountifully spread table, supplied with seasonable fish, fowl, fruit and vegetables from the great lake and the immediate countryside. Fresh cream, eggs, milk and butter go far to make the menu most delightful.

— Grand Traverse, the Summer Land, 1910

New Riverside Inn

The Riverside Inn

A fine addition to the beauty spots of Leland and to the hotel advantages of this region is the new "Riverside Inn" built last summer to replace the one that burned the year before. This new structure is prettily situated between the bank of the river and River Street. It is modern in every respect and is newly furnished throughout. This hotel will open for the season under the firm name of Schwartz Sisters. The firm consists of Miss Anna Schwartz and Mrs. Blanche Scott. Their fine equipment and experience is sufficient guarantee of a pleasant place to stay and satisfactory table service.

— Leelanau Enterprise, April 22, 1926

BLUE LANTERN TEA ROOM, LELAND, MICH.

Blue Lantern Tea Room is Popular

Here is one of the most attractive places to stop for lunch, tea or dinner. The tea room is gay with brightly painted furniture, color-ful hangings, and nicely appointed table service. Meals are served in the tea house, on the porch and on the lawn under bright sun-umbrellas. The food is always delicious. Mrs. Maro raises all of her own vegetables, to be sure of getting fresh foods for her tables.

The cottages that Mrs. Maro has to rent are equipped for every need. Screened porches, electric cooking plates, baths, fireplaces, and a radio in each cottage.

The tea room and cottages are on a beautifully landscaped site on Lake Leelanau. The shore of the lake is sandy and provides good swimming. There are lots of flowers, shrubs and trees.

The absolute cleanliness of the place is one of its many charms.

— Traverse City Record Eagle, June 29, 1931

ADVERTISEMENT — BLUE LANTERN TEA ROOM

— Traverse City Record Eagle, 1931

When in the Grand Traverse Region, Phone Mrs. Maro
after July First at

The Blue Lantern Tea Room
(EIGHTH SEASON)

In Leland and make an appointment for Luncheon, Dinner or Bridge Parties. Then follow M-22 from Traverse City to a mile north of Leland post office. Look for the sign and THE BLUE LANTERN by the road side. Turn into the field and follow on to a nice surprise.

Of Course, there's Afternoon Tea

Leland, Michigan, is 25 miles north and west of Traverse City, on Lake Michigan and Lake Leelanau.

Many choice lots for summer homes for sale adjoining Tea Room properties. Furnished Cottages for rent by the season.

Good Roads In All Directions

BLUEBIRD FINE EATING PLACE

No vacation is a really restful one when you are held in leash by lack of a place where you can relax and enjoy yourself, a place where you cast off the shackles of workaday worries.

Located in the village of Leland on the banks of the Leelanau River, the Bluebird Tavern serves meals and refreshments. Overlooking the river is a spacious dance floor. Music is furnished by an excellent orchestra and the management is always ready to offer those little hospitalities that are usually lost in the shuffle of commercialization.

Whether it is a cup of coffee that you want, or an entire evening of fun, you will do well to take into consideration the Bluebird Tavern. You will find your friends there.

A specialty at the tavern that is gaining justly deserved fame is the fried lake trout dinner. Crisp brown pieces of delicate fish served with all the generosity of a country home is a treat that will never be forgotten. Homemade pies are also served in the tavern which, under the management of Mr. and Mrs. Martin Telegard, is rapidly becoming a popular spot in Leelanau County.

— *Traverse City Record Eagle,* June 25, 1940

ADVERTISEMENT — BLUE BIRD RESTAURANT
— *Leland Resort Directory,* 1937

ADVERTISEMENT — BLUE BIRD TAVERN
— *Traverse City Record Eagle,* 1940

The Nicholas,
Leland, Mich.

Nicholas Hotel Fine Hostelry

One of the most inspiring views of the entire Grand Traverse region can be had from the spacious front porch of the Nicholas Hotel in Leland. Here, on a promontory that juts high above its surroundings is located a modern hostelry that offers everything in the way of a splendid vacation.

Cool in the summer because of the ever present breeze that sweeps in from Lake Michigan, yet not too cool to be uncomfortable, the hotel is fast approaching a position of great importance in the minds of those who like a restful vacation.

The spacious dining room in connection with the hotel seats 500 people. Rachel's Tea Room, overlooking Lake Leelanau, offers a la carte service in a pleasant atmosphere.

Cool evenings are tempered by a spacious fireplace in the hotel, and over all is that blanket of friendliness that is so essential to a good vacation. Available in the community is a fine beach, yacht club, golf course, and countless other scenes of activity. Frank Rossman, who has been a host of the past 30 years, has made thousands of friends, testimonials to the excellence of his service.

— *Traverse City Record Eagle,* June 25, 1940

We are sure you'd like the service
 And the atmosphere as well,
That is offered to the patrons
 Of the Nicholas Hotel.

The food is really excellent,
 There's joy in every bite—
And the northern air is tonic
 For a jaded appetite.

There is tennis, golf and bathing;
 You may sail, or swim, or rest;
We will prove, if you will join us,
 That the Nicholas is best.

"TAKE THINE EASE; EAT, DRINK AND BE MERRY"
at
The New Nicholas Hotel
Pleasantly located on an elevation overlooking the blue waters of Lake Michigan and Lake Leelanau.
GOLF   TENNIS
FISHING   BATHING   MOTOR AND
                                        SAIL BOATING
Dining Room Seats 500 » Always Cool
Rachel's Tea Room connected with Hotel
(May be reached over Scenic Highway M-22)
F. P. Rosman, Proprietor
                                        Leland, Mich.

Above: ADVERTISEMENT — THE NICHOLAS (POEM) — *Traverse City Record Eagle,* 1938
Right: ADVERTISEMENT — THE NEW NICHOLAS HOTEL — *Michigan Scenic Highways,* 1933

Leland Lodge In Picturesque Leland

The Leland Lodge plays host to hundreds who annually trek north to enjoy the carefree days of their vacation. Located equi-distant from the shores of Lake Michigan and Lake Leelanau, Leland Lodge is ideally situated to offer the most beautiful landscape and cool breezes that are such a welcome summer refreshment.

Many years of resort management insures that your stay at Leland Lodge will be the vacation of a lifetime…a wholesome, refreshing period away from the routine of everyday life among interesting new people. Plan now to let us entertain you this summer and guarantee yourself a delightful experience…

Realizing how necessary good food is to a happy vacation, we have made every effort to insure your culinary enjoyment by providing not only the best of menus but clean, comfortable dining facilities with just the right atmosphere…

Season June 10 to September 15

American and European Plan

Lodge and Guest Cottages

— *Leland Lodge, circa* 1958

25th Year for the Swiss Inn

Entering its 25th year as a summer resort, the Swiss Inn, located on M-22 one-half mile south of Leland and but an hour's drive from Traverse City, is ideally adapted to serve summer visitors.

Besides the spacious lodge there are three cottages located nearby. Each is well equipped with electricity and running water. The main building is built in Swiss style with a low slanting roof and numerous gables. It is stucco with brown trimming. There are fifteen sleeping rooms. A large dining room opens off a screened porch that runs the width of the building.

George Paige, former Traverse City man and proprietor of the Inn makes a specialty of his home cooked fish, steak and chicken dinners. There is room for dancing.

Situated but 200 feet from Lake Leelanau, the spot is ideal for those wishing to try their skill against the countless game fish in the waters of the lake harbor. The management will provide fishing tackle for those who don't happen to have any with them. A new dock has been built at the foot of the property and three power launches and a number of row boats are ready to be utilized.

— *Traverse City Record Eagle,* June 30, 1935

On all sides of the village of Leland are cottage colonies, north, south and east. The term "cottage" does not indicate in this case, a small summer place, but has grown to be used to mean any summer dwelling. But the Leland summer homes are outstanding in their architecture and design. In fact, many of them are mansions.

— *Traverse City Record Eagle*, July 31, 1926

A Beautiful Garden

Leelanau County in Resort Boom
Large Building Program Is On As
Summer Colony Enters Best Year

Leland, July 7 — With summer homes of more than $250,000 value under construction, Leelanau County is entering into its greatest year as a summer colony. More than $100,000 in new buildings are nearing completion in the Leland vicinity alone, while Northport, Lake Leelanau, Sutton's Bay and Glen Arbor report large operations.

Few of the cottages are large, according to contractors, who estimate the average cost is in the vicinity of $7,000. Although the resort season was very late in starting, hotels and cottages have been filling up in the past few days and a record crowd is expected by the middle of the month.

— *Grand Rapids Press*, July 7, 1926

Birchcroft Hotel

Birchcroft Hotel is well-patronized this season by resorters, running to its capacity. Fishing parties are enjoying rare sport these days, many fine catches of the finny tribe being made.

— *Leelanau Enterprise*, August 11, 1919

Artist at Leland

The Artist's Wonderland…Annually Leelanau County attracts hundreds of artists and art students. The fishing fleet at Leland is one of their favored spots as is the giant Sleeping Bear, the panorama from atop the hills overlooking Glen Lake, Lake Michigan, and the North and South Manitou Islands in Lake Michigan is also a lure to the artist.

— Vacation Days in Michigan's Grand Traverse Bay Region,
Traverse City Area Chamber of Commerce, 1961

The Leland Yacht Club was organized in 1936 and served as the focal point for water sports on Lake Leelanau. Since its beginning, sailing had long been the favorite and most extensive activity of the club. The Club sponsored sailing regattas throughout the summer and drew many spectators to watch the events.

This seasoned fisherman may recall the heyday of Leland's fishing industry when as many as eight commercial fishing boats operated out of Leland and whitefish, trout, and chub were caught by the ton. Fishtown's colorful history has long been a "lure" for tourists.

Leland Country Club

Leland Country Club, Leland, Mich.

Play Excellent Golf on a Well Kept Course

Lying on the edge of Leland, and available for all the Lake Leelanau district, is the Leland Country Club with its excellent nine-hole golf club where some of the best golf of the north is played every season.

The Leland club is made up largely of cottagers who come back to Leland year after year, entranced with its summer season. By liberal expenditure of money they have laid out a course second to none in the region and one which never becomes tiresome.

From time to time during the summer, real golfers drop in and play the Leland course. College players who rank with the best amateurs of the United States, are there during the summer, and Chicago, Cincinnati, Louisville, and Detroit furnish talent which is seldom seen outside the city courses.

The Leland club plays inter-resort tournaments during the summer, usually playing home matches with the summer folks which would make the average professional jealous.

— *Leelanau Enterprise*, July 31, 1926

Leland Golf Club

Offers you a
Speedy 9-Hole Golf Course
Wonderful Views
Moderate Greens Fee
Club House Conveniences
Soft Drinks and Lunches
LELAND, MICH.

ADVERTISEMENT — LELAND GOLF CLUB
— "Vacation Handbook and Fisherman's Guide, Leelanau County," *Leelanau Enterprise*, 1942

ADVERTISEMENT — LELAND COUNTRY CLUB
— "Road Map & Business Directory of Leelanau County,"
Leelanau Enterprise, 1925

The
Leland Country Club
at Leland, Michigan

offers a sporty nine hole course, situated on a rolling elevation between Lake Michigan and Lake Leelanau, where golf may be enjoyed, with natural beauty on every hand.

Every shot presents a picture of blue water and wooded hillside. The putting greens are turf--kept in the best possible condition.

Frequent and varied tournaments stimulate interest in the game.

Excellent Clay Tennis Courts

The privileges of the Golf Course and Tennis Courts are available on a Moderate Green fee basis.

Northport & Northport Point

Northport

Northport is beautifully situated on the eastern side, near the tip of the Leelanau Peninsula, on the shores of Grand Traverse Bay, about 28 miles north of Traverse City.

Northport was originally called Waukazooville, after Chief Peter Waukazoo, who with the Reverend George Smith, brought 40 or 50 Native American families to Leelanau County from the Holland area in 1849. He was accompanied by James McLaughlin, who had been working with Smith as a teacher of farming to the Native Americans. Five years later Deacon Joseph Dame and his son platted the present village, which he named Northport. In 1855 the United States government recognized the Grand Traverse Ottawa and Chippewa Reservation in Leelanau Township, but excluded the village of Northport from the reservation boundaries.

Joseph Dame was one of the earliest promoters of Leelanau County. In January of 1854 he wrote a letter to the *New York Tribune* giving a glowing description of the Grand Traverse region. The letter was published in March, and when Deacon Dame picked up his mail the following month, he received 64 letters of inquiry about the new country, and soon pioneers were coming to the area.

The early pioneers landed at Northport's natural harbor. The village life was centered on the harbor's activity. Northport was an important port of call for schooners and steamers on the Buffalo-Detroit-Chicago run. In 1852 the first lighthouse, originally called Cat's Head Light, was erected eight miles north of Northport at the tip of the peninsula. This first structure was replaced in 1864 with a brick building, which included living quarters for the keeper. A fog signal building was added in 1899. The safety that that the lighthouse ensured greatly contributed to the development of Northport's harbor and eventually four docks were built to accommodate the thriving wooding business. When coal replaced wood as the fuel for most steamships, the wooding business was supplanted by the sawmill business. Northport's docks continued to be busy with shipments of lumber, fish, farm and fruit products.

The first cherries were grown by the Reverend George Smith, who bought his first cherry trees in 1853. The climate proved ideal for growing cherries, and soon other pioneers followed his success. In the 1910s several cherry orchards were developed, but it was in the 1920s and 1930s that large-scale cherry farming was established. The largest producer was the Cherry Home Orchard. For many years it was the world's largest red tart cherry producer. Cherry Home had its own dock, warehouse, canning factory, and dormitories.

Northport had an active commercial fishing industry. By 1880 whitefish, lake trout, and chub were sold commercially. At the fishing industry's height, eight fishing rigs operated out of Northport.

Northport was a thriving village by 1900 with two hotels, a restaurant, post office, school, telephone service, several businesses, and three docks. Northport was sometimes referred to as the "Great Emporium" of the north. The Traverse City, Leelanau and Manistique Railroad arrived in Northport in June of 1903 — a festive occasion for the townspeople. Within the year, railroad car ferry service was established to Manistique. The *Manistique, Marquette and Northern No. One* operated from 1903 to 1908 transporting both freight cars and people to the Upper Peninsula.

Before the tourist business took hold, Northport provided food and lodging for many visitors traveling by steamship. Joseph Dame accommodated early transients in his home, but soon built a hotel, the Exchange, at the foot of his dock. By 1860 a larger hotel was needed and he built the Traverse Bay Hotel, which changed hands several times and later operated as the Waukazoo until it burned in 1902. Other early hotels included the Porter House (later called the Hotel Scott), the Bayview House, and the Osabewinning Hotel. The largest of the summer resort hotels was the Northport Beach Hotel, with 110 guest rooms and accommodations for 250 guests. It was built in 1903, but burned only five years later, in 1908. The hotel was not rebuilt, as the owners had no insurance on the building.

Several boarding houses also served the needs of the traveling public. One of the earliest was the Budd House, which operated until the late 1940s. The Hotel Northern operated from 1920 to 1970 with nine rooms for guests. In the 1930s and 1940s the Willowbrook Inn and Bayview Tourist Home offered overnight accommodations. With increased automobile touring, tourist camps and cabins

A Picnic Celebration at Northport, circa 1900

became popular. The Homewood Cabins opened in 1939 and the Bayshore Cabins in 1945. As time went on, many visitors returned to the Northport area to build summer homes.

The 1930s and 1940s brought added attractions to the Northport area. The Clinton F. Woolsey Memorial Airport was built in 1935 and accommodated those summer visitors with private planes. Five miles north of Northport, George Raff opened his "Deep Sea Fishing Camp." Tourists were promised phenomenal catches of trout by trolling. By 1955 Raff had cabins, a campground, a dining room, and 25 powerboats with guides. Customers caught huge lake trout weighing up to 45 pounds. For years Raff's promotional slogan was "no trout, no pay." In 1932 the government gave 30 acres at the Grand Traverse Lighthouse to the Conservation Department for use as a state park. The lighthouse continued to operate until 1972, when the light was automated and moved to a steel tower on the shore. The Grand Traverse Lighthouse, now adjacent to the state park, is currently a museum operated by the Grand Traverse Lighthouse Foundation.

Northport, Mich., looking S. W.

*Northport, Michigan
looking Southwest*

Northport, one of the older villages in Leelanau County, furnishes many attractions for summer resorters. On high land, sloping eastward towards the bay, surrounded by a country that furnishes ample supplies of fresh vegetables, butter, milk, eggs and all kinds of excellent fruit, with the combined attractions of good fishing and bathing, cool springs and pure air from the water, Northport is a well-endowed resort.

The winter population of the village is about four hundred, which in summer is increased to about five to six hundred, by the visitors and resorters. The water supply is from drive wells, and springs, which are plentiful, and the hotels furnish good accommodations to visitors. The resort is accessible by the Detroit and Cleveland, the Northern Michigan, and the Traverse Bay lines of boats, and often from fifteen to twenty-five boats touch there every week.

— Michigan: a Summer and Health Resort State, 1898

The location of Northport is interesting and peculiar. The harbor is one of the most commodious on the lakes. The village is built upon terraces, and has somewhat the look of a rural village in New England. The surrounding farming country is excellent, but limited in extent, as less than three miles distant to the west is the shore of Lake Michigan.

— *Traverse Region, Historical and Descriptive,* 1884

Northport Village — *Beautifully situated on the eastern side of the Leelanau peninsula and on the shore of the Grand Traverse Bay, it offers the most excellent advantage to seekers for health, wealth, and happiness. In the heart of a most thriving and prosperous farm section, fresh fruit, eggs, poultry, and produce can be gotten every day from the local dealers to supply the voracious appetites of summer visitors. It is now provided with all the conveniences to be found in a modern village, telephones, telegraph, two daily mails, hotels, stores, livery barns, pleasure boats, and in fact all the necessary advantages to a summer outing. This is a pretty spot as those who have viewed it from the bay can attest. It has a population of about 500, good schools, churches, and is a moral law abiding community. There is no saloon in the village and none nearer than twelve miles — an ideal spot to spend the summer with a family of children.*

— *Beauty Spots in Leelanau,* 1901 *Souvenir*

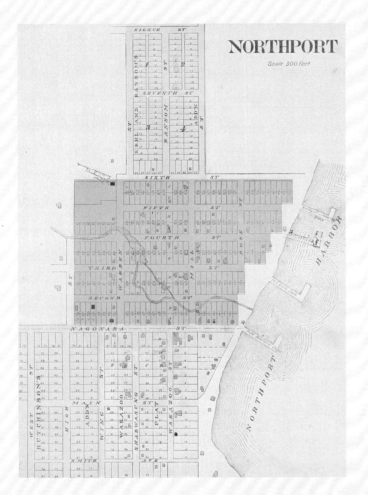

NORTHPORT

Scale 300 feet

Nagonaba Street

MAP OF NORTHPORT, *Atlas of Leelanau County*, 1900

Northport is located near the tip of the Leelanau Peninsula, 11 miles north of Leland and 30 miles north of Traverse City. In 1900 Northport had a population of 500. It had a Methodist, a Congregational, and two Lutheran churches, and a graded school. Daily stage service traveled to Omena, Suttons Bay, Keswick, Bingham, Norrisville and Traverse City. Triweekly stage service went to Gill's Pier, Leland, Good Harbor, Shetland, North Unity, Glen Arbor, Port Oneida, and Glen Haven. In 1900 Northport had two hotels, a lumber company, a gristmill, a general store, a butcher, a restaurant, three carpenters, a blacksmith, two physicians, a cornet band, and a telephone company.

The village of Northport has one of the best harbors in Grand Traverse Bay
and has railroad facilities over the Grand Rapids and Indiana line. With active flour and lumber mills,
still maintaining quite a fishing trade, and backed by a country which is productive of fruit, vegetables, seeds and grain. Northport
is becoming one of the most promising centers of population in Leelanau county. The village transacts its business through the
Leelanau County Bank, enjoys electric lighting and shows its moral stamina by supporting six religious organizations —
one Methodist, one Congregational, one Catholic, one Swedish Mission, and two Norwegian Lutheran.

— Powers, *A History of Northern Michigan*, 1912

Northport Has Vacation Lure

Thirty miles from Traverse City on M–22 is one of the finest resort towns in the Grand Traverse Bay region. In the early days of this locality, Northport was a harbor and fishing terminal at the northern tip of Leelanau County and this fame has been adhered to until the present time. Several stores, tourist homes and service stations make up the business section of the village. Everything is up–to–date and the folks have a friendly air about them.

In a shady grove just off the main highway, is a tourist camp known as Siesta Park. Various forms of recreation can be enjoyed there. Two shuffleboard courts, tennis courts and a croquet court are facilities at the disposal of visitors. Every Saturday evening the community band plays a concert at this site.

Since the decline of commercial fishing and lumbering the community has taken new life with their cherry orchards and added tourist trade. These comparatively new industries place the little city in a conspicuous spot in the general layout of the Grand Traverse region.

— Traverse City Record Eagle, June 30, 1935

Hay fever is unknown in Northport and the sweet odor of the balsam and cedar is in itself a source of health.

— Michigan in Summer, 1910

Inn's a Regular Stopping Place

Summer tourists in the vicinity of Northport find the Willow Brook Tea Room and Inn a homelike place amid pleasant surroundings. Located beside a babbling brook stands the huge willow tree from whence came the name of the hostelry. Beneath the tree is a rock garden harboring a variety of lovely flowers. Another feature of the surroundings is a miniature water wheel.

Since 1931 the tea room has been operated by Mrs. R.E. Campbell and many summer guests make it a regular stopping place. The reputation of the Willow Brook is based on splendid home cooking expertly prepared.

— *Traverse City Record Eagle,* June 30, 1935

Eat Beside the Running Brook

Willow Brook Tea Room and Inn

Where Every Bite Is Just Right

HOME MADE FUDGE
CAKES AND PIES TO ORDER   NORTHPORT, MICH.

Advertisement — Willow Brook Tea Room

— *Traverse City Record Eagle,* 1935

Dear Aunt Ida,

Rode up here today with some people from Old Mission Inn. We are having our lunch here. We are sitting in a screened in porch with a brook running along side. We haven't eaten yet so can not say how the food is. But the smells are good.

— Marie

Postmarked Northport, 1947
Mailed to Kansas City, Missouri.

The Northern Popular Place

Hotel Northern at Northport has evolved within the past few years from a hostelry catering almost exclusively to commercial trade into a very popular summer hotel.

Bert Ellis laid aside his chef's apron three years ago, purchased and took over the management of the Hotel Northern. He has had splendid success in his venture and Hotel Northern has become as an important a summer hotel as it is a commercial hotel in winter. Mr. Ellis has enlarged considerably the accommodations of the hotel and has held to a high standard of meals and service.

The hotel is on the main highway entering Northport and while its guests have convenient access to the bay shore they are not only within the village limits but are handily located near principal stores.

Hotel Northern is a favorite stopping place for campers touring Leelanau County.

— Traverse City Record Eagle, June 27, 1927

Beautiful Place is Budd Cottage

Standing at the corner of two picturesquely, Indian-name streets — Stabawasung and Nagonaba — is the Budd Cottage, for over a quarter of a century a landmark in Northport. Surrounding the comfortable looking home are giant maple trees offering cool shelter from a hot summer sun. At the door you are met by a little lady, who shows a great deal of hospitality and consideration for your every want, during a delicious dinner or luncheon. Should you tarry longer your hostess will show you to comfortable rooms furnished in good taste.

— Traverse City Record Eagle, June 30, 1935

Northports' Indian Craft Shop At M22 & M201 Junction Prop. Jessie W. Hilton~ Grandaughter of Rev. Geo. N. Smith, Founder of Northport, Mich

Jessie   Lucille

Indian Crafts and Souvenirs

Native Americans found a ready market for their crafts with tourists looking for a souvenir to bring home. The Indian Craft shop, above, offered "guaranteed genuine handicraft" including baskets and moccasins. The Cedar Chest, to right, offered Indian crafts, souvenirs, and postcards.

Chest~ Northport Mich. 3271

A Scene at the Fishing Docks –
Northport Mich.

Northport is a quiet and healthful place. The cool breezes from the surrounding water blow gently day and
night through all the summer, making it a most desirable spot for those seeking rest and a change from the
heat and dust of the city.

As to climate, scientists making tests have discovered that this region stands second to none in the
amount of ozone in the atmosphere, as measured by the Ozonemeter, so this little peninsula can well be
advertised as a health resort — a place where one can sleep well all night and wake up with a ravenous
appetite ready to partake of the well-cooked wholesome food, fresh home-grown vegetables, fruits, eggs,
sweet cream and butter, and milk that bubbles in the pail.

— *Traverse City Record Eagle,* July 28, 1938

HOMEWOOD CABINS NORTHPORT, MICH. 450·8

Dear Folks:

The time is going too fast, but we are having a grand time. How cool it is today. Hope you are having some of this cool breeze. The men are out fishing, and the lake is so wavy. We've had one good fish dinner. I went along with them Thursday, but my legs got so sun-burned and sore that I'm staying near the cottage for a couple of days. I think they tried to cure me of wanting to go fishing. We drove to Traverse City yesterday, and took in the sights. Another friend arrived today to spend a week with us. We eat too much, I'm getting fat I know.

— Lillian

Postmark not legible, circa 1940
Mailed to Rockford, Illinois

Homewood Cabins

The Air Port
NorthPort Mich

C-7157

WOOLSEY AIR PORT   NORTH PORT POINT, MICH.   C-1602

Woolsey's Air Port

The only airport in Leelanau County is located at Northport.
It is called the Clinton Woolsey Airport and is named for Captain
Woolsey who lost his life in a Good Will flight to South America in
February 1927. The land was donated by the aviator's father,
Byron Woolsey, and was part of the farm on which Clinton was
born. The airport was dedicated on July 14, 1935. The first letters
to be carried by Air Mail from Northport were picked up on
May 19, 1938, in honor of Byron Woolsey's 88th birthday.

—"Vacation Handbook and Fisherman's
Guide, Leelanau County,"
Leelanau Enterprise, 1940

Norman Furst Guide   Cabin Boats at Raff's Trout Camp Northport Mich   N...

Raff's Trout Camp

George Raff's Mackinaw Fishing Camp: *Stay as long as you wish...we have excellent accommodations. To make your visit extra pleasant, we have made our camp such that you will be more than pleased to stay. We have everything you need for your convenience and a little extra for good measure.*

Our grounds are, of course, situated right on the most beautiful bay in the world, but besides this, the entire camp grounds as well as the surrounding part of the peninsula on which we are located is heavily wooded with Northern pines, etc. Here is your opportunity to enjoy a real restful sleep. Our camp is different from the ordinary tourist camp where large crowds and noise predominate, but here you will find absolute quiet after sunset except for the gentle breaking of the waves on shore and the wind sighing in the trees.

We are adding new cabins every year, cabins with good, clean easy beds that will induce absolute rest and comfort. Electric lights, telephone, in fact all conveniences and yet secluded — a rare combination these days when most camps cater to as large a crowd as possible.

Excellent bathing beach — one of the best in Michigan.

On the other hand, you are also near to those famous Northern hotels where deluxe facilities are available so close to the natural.

— George Raff's Mackinaw Fishing Camp, circa 1930

George Raff Fishing Camp

WHERE THE BIG ONES ARE CAUGHT

DEEP SEA
FISHING

is the Sport of Sports

You'll get the thrill of a lifetime in bringing in these huge Mackinaw Trout from the depths of Lake Michigan.....You don't even have to know how to fish.....Capable, experienced guides in sturdy, seaworthy boats teach you the simple technique, and the fun and the trophies are yours..... Women and children enjoy it too!

Open Boats $1.25 per hour.   Cabin Boats $1.50 per hour.
As many can go as the boat will hold at no extra cost.

CABINS and DINING ROOM SERVICE at the camp site.   PHONE 5-F4

Just Follow the Blue Arrows from Northport, Mich.

ADVERTISEMENT — GEORGE RAFF FISHING CAMP

— Traverse City Record Eagle, 1937

Raff's Fishing Resort was located on Crystal Cove, five miles north of Northport. In the mid-1930s the resort had two permanent residences, several guest cabins, a camping area, a restaurant, and 23 charter boats.

Raff's Mackinaw Trout Camp Northport Mich

Bluffs, Lake Michigan, Northport

On the west side of Northport Point are the beautiful bluffs which rise abruptly 200 feet above Lake Michigan, overlooking the lighthouse and Cathead Bay, the grand and stately Manitou and Fox Islands, and commanding a magnificent view, where large vessels are constantly passing to and fro.

— Traverse City Record Eagle, June 20, 1931

The Log Cabin at the Bluffs, Northport, Mich.

Log Cabin at the Bluffs

Log Cabin Has Lure For Many

Overlooking Lake Michigan, two hundred feet above the water sits the "Log Cabin" at "The Bluffs." For fifteen years, while less fortunate folks have been sweltering in the cities, smarter people have visited the "Log Cabin" to partake of one of the chicken, fish or steak dinners for which it is so noted, and at the same time exalt in the cool, refreshing breezes which are wafted over the place from the lake.

The "Log Cabin" is located a few miles northwest of Northport, on the opposite side of the peninsula. Situated in this high spot, in a gathering of birch trees, and overlooking the Fox and Manitou Islands in the distance, this homey little cabin has long been a favorite hideaway for the most prominent of Northern Michigan's resort visitors.

By means of raising their own vegetables, fruit and farm produce, the Garthes have acquired that "Home baked" touch in the preparation of their foods, capturing the fancy of all those who visit. Dinners are served by appointment only.

— Traverse City Record Eagle, June 30, 1933

The Log Cabin at the Bluffs, Northport, Mich.

Advertisement — The Log Cabin

— "Vacation Handbook and Fisherman's Guide,"
Leelanau Enterprise, 1938

Northport Point

Northport Point is a narrow strip of land jutting out into Grand Traverse Bay, just north of the village of Northport. The Native Americans called it "O-ne-ka-win," or carrying point. The natives often portaged their canoes across this narrow strip of land to save a few miles of paddling. Carrying Point later became a favorite picnic spot for local people and summer visitors.

In 1899 Carrying Point was sold to Orin Ward and George Winnans. They changed the name to Northport Point and platted the land for summer cottages. A dock was built on the harbor side to accommodate the Traverse Bay Line of steamers. Ward and Winnans opened their summer resort hotel, the Cedar Lodge, in 1900. The hotel had 54 rooms, a dining room, electric lights and telephones. An addition was built the following year and more rooms were added.

Some of the early guests of the Cedar Lodge purchased lots and built cottages at Northport Point. Orin Ward organized the Northport Point Resort Association, which assisted in the development of the summer resort. In 1914 cottage owners on the Point formed the Northport Point Golf and Country Club. The Northport Point Cottage Owners Association was incorporated in 1915 to provide the necessary functions such as fire and police protection, water supply, road maintenance, and garbage removal. The Atwill Memorial Chapel was completed in 1912 and named in honor of Bishop Edward R. Atwill and his wife who had served at Northport Point. The nonsectarian chapel was built with a rustic beauty that befitted its sylvan setting. In 1922 the Association built the Leelanau Golf Course. The private summer colony prospered, and has some of the county's most beautiful homes. Many have been in the same family for generations. In 1960 the Association demolished and carefully burned the Cedar Lodge to make a beach park for cottagers on the Point.

MAP *Northport Area Vacation at Northport*, circa 1940

This promotional map of the Northport area shows some of the popular attractions for visitors, including Northport Point Resort, Leelanau Golf Club, the Mackinaw trolling grounds, Woolsey Airport, the Grand Traverse Lighthouse, Omena Resort, and the Indian village of Peshawbestown.

O-Ne-Ka-Win

This historic spot probably has more Indian lore connected with it than falls to the lot of most summer resorts. The name O-Ne-Ka-Win is the Ojibway word for Carrying Point, meaning more properly a clearing across the land, or an opening to let in light. It was so named from the fact that a lone Indian many years before any of the present tribe have any record of, came and settled on the point and cleared off the land at the narrowest place and tilled the soil, raising corn and such. The Indians, in passing up and down the bay, discovered this spot and found it a much shorter route to the mainland, and they used to go ashore here and carry their canoes across the narrow strip of land where the fine Cedar Hotel now stands. The little peninsula is nearly two miles in length from where it joins the mainland and is heavily wooded with evergreens, poplars, beech, maple, etc. The shores are sandy and slope gently to the waters edge making it an ideal shore for bathing purposes.

— Beauty Spots in Leelanau, 1901 Souvenir

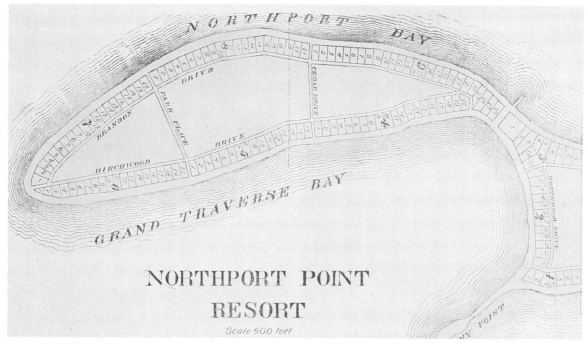

MAP OF NORTHPORT POINT, *Atlas of Leelanau County*, 1900

This map of Northport Point shows the proposed lots for the popular summer resort colony that would soon follow.
The Cedar Lodge opened in 1900 and was an immediate success. Lots were sold, and cottages were built soon after.

Northport Point — *This resort has already become famous for the quiet beauty of its natural surroundings. The shores are ideal; in the hottest summer weather there always seems to be a breeze. Bathing is unexcelled. There is a broad, sandy beach where the water deepens gradually, and is protected from the north by Stony Point, which keeps the waters warm.*

— *Michigan in Summer,* 1904

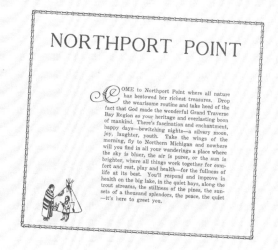

NORTHPORT POINT

COME to Northport Point where all nature has bestowed her richest treasures. Drop the wearisome routine and take heed of the fact that God made the wonderful Grand Traverse Bay Region as your heritage and everlasting boon of mankind. There's fascination and enchantment, happy days—bewitching nights—a silvery moon, joy, laughter, youth. Take the wings of the morning, fly to Northern Michigan and nowhere will you find in all your wanderings a place where the sky is bluer, the air is purer, or the sun is brighter, where all things work together for comfort and rest, play and health—for the fullness of life at its best. You'll respond and improve in health on the big lake, in the quiet bays, along the trout streams, the stillness of the pines, the sunsets of a thousand splendors, the peace, the quiet —it's here to greet you.

Cedar Lodge

Among the coming summer resorts of the north is Northport, in beautiful Leelanau County. Here in one of the most exceptionally well chosen spots is located the new summer resort hotel, "Cedar Lodge," constructed by mine host Fred. H. Giddings. "Cedar Lodge," an ideal summer hotel of the most modern type with 100 guest rooms and up-to-date improvements, stands on Northport Point, a narrow strip of land jutting out into the bay and forming a lagoon or height, as it is called. It is on the narrowest point on this strip that "Cedar Lodge" is located. The dining room will seat 150 people. A fine water works system, telephones, mails twice each day, boat livery, fine bathing beach, fishing, etc. are some of the facilities at this pretty hotel. Rates are exceedingly modest for the excellent service, ranging at $1.50 per day and $7.00 to $10.00 per week. Mr. Giddings will be pleased to answer all inquiries regarding rooms, etc.

— *Grand Rapids Evening Press,* June 29, 1901

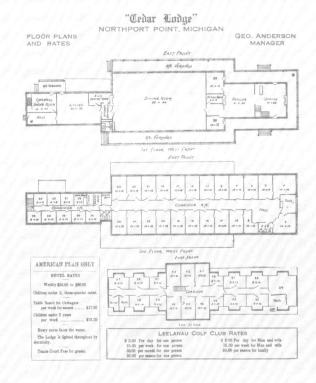

Cedar Lodge Floor Plan — Cedar Lodge, Northport Point, circa 1930

The Cedar Lodge has fifty rooms, every one facing the water. It is
equipped throughout with electric lights. The dining room is on
the ground floor and a beautiful view of the Bay is obtained from
every seat. The fame of the Cedar Lodge, justly achieved, is based
on the merits of its cuisine and attention bestowed upon the guests.
The comforts and enjoyment are sufficient to warrant a stay
for the entire summer.

— *Grand Traverse Region*, circa 1914

Dining Room, Cedar Lodge, Northport Point, Mich.

Cedar Lodge

Cedar Lodge
Northport Point Mich.

Northport Point is one of the most healthful places in Michigan,
absolutely free from malaria and a paradise for hay-fever sufferers.

An abundance of pure water is assured. The sanitary conditions
are under personal supervision and maintained to the highest standards
by rigidly enforced rules.

The many excellent farms adjoining the Point supply the cottagers
and Lodge with fresh fruits, vegetables, milk, butter, eggs, etc. Fresh
lake trout and whitefish are served daily.

Northport Point is not an ultra fashionable place; you can enjoy
your vacation without the tiresome exactions and unwelcome demands
which are so often made on one's time and purse at resorts where
society is made the most prominent feature.

Come to enjoy the summer. Come to find health in the woods
and on the water, and go back to your work with the exhilaration and
renewed vigor that results from association with nature where the
very air is a tonic, and the surroundings an inspiration.

— *Cedar Lodge, Northport Point*, circa 1930

Northport Point, Mich.

This is the cottage we are
spending a month. Look out
6 miles across Traverse Bay. A
wonderful spot. Dense woods
back of us with all kinds of
ferns and moss. Am sending a
box of Kinnicinik. Love to all.

— Marie

Postmarked Northport Point, 1921
Mailed to Brooklyn, New York

Birchmere Cottage

The earliest cottage on Northport Point
was built by Orin Ward in 1900.
He named it "Birchmere" because
of the birch trim used throughout
the cottage. East and West porches
offered magnificent views of the
sunrise amd sunset.

Northport Summer People Have Two Golf Courses

No territory in Northern Michigan holds forth more promise to the lover of golf than Northport Point where two excellent courses give a variety of play found nowhere else in Michigan.

The Northport Point Resort Association has just completed a most attractively planned nine-hole, rolling golf course, 3,366 yards long, called the Leelanau Golf Club, designed by Jack L. Daray, golf architect, professional at Olympian Fields, Homewood, Ill. This club has been developed for the guests of the Cedar Lodge and cottagers who plan to make Northport their summer home. Situated on a commanding elevation overlooking Grand Traverse Bay, Northport Point, Paradesia Point, Seven Pines and the Golf Links, is a charming log cabin club-house with a low sweeping roof, appropriate great low stone chimney with fireplace. Nothing more suitable or picturesque could have been devised for the comfort of members and their guests.

The Leelanau Golf Club, one of the most interesting and intriguing to be found among the resorts, is laid out in a sightly spot overlooking two bodies of water. The nearness of the cooling bays is guarantee of golf weather every day of the summer season. The course is in excellent condition this year and has been pronounced one of the sportiest in the north.

In addition to its own two courses, the region is so located that a short drive will bring the golf enthusiast to other excellent courses. Leland, Omena, Glen Lake and Traverse City are but a short, pleasant drive from the Northport district and all of these places have golf courses.

— *Traverse City Record Eagle*, July 30, 1926

Dock and Store

The dock and store at Northport Point were the social center of life for many years. Many summer afternoons found young "Pointers" enjoying ice cream or soda pop from the concession.

The Northport Beach Hotel is one of the most modern of the Northern Michigan resorts. It is lathed and plastered and has double floors throughout. Electric light, steam heat and telephone in every room. Accommodations for 250 guests.

— *Northport Beach Hotel*, Northport, Michigan, 1902

Northport Beach Hotel

North port Beach Hotel, North port, Mich.

Printed in Germany.

Northport Beach is a new resort and will be ready for visitors this summer. There are one hundred and fifty acres, heavily wooded, on the shores of Northport Bay, a short distance north of Northport Village.

The Northport Beach Hotel is a new hotel of modern appointments. Every care has been taken to make this hotel comfortable and first-class in every way. It is two hundred and fifteen feet long and has one hundred and ten rooms for guests.

— *Michigan in Summer*, 1903

Dear Nellie,

How are you all. We are well. I got your card. Sweet cherries sell for 7 1/2 cents a lb. Sours for 4 cents a lb. It is raining nearly all day. Hope it gets rained out by tomorrow. We have good picking now and ever so many come here and want pickers. I picked 9 lugs yesterday and Ma 8. Tomorrow we are going where they are lots bigger. The wind has spoiled a lot of them. I wish some of you were here, you could make some money. We want to go through the canning factory when it stops raining. Ask Mabel to show you the boat we sent her. The rent check comes separate. We might stay two weeks yet. By By.

(Write)

— Amanda

Postmarked from Northport, 1937
Mailed to Harrison, Michigan

Northport Has Great Orchard
Cherry Home is Biggest Cherry Sour Cherry Block in World

Near Northport is Cherry Home, the biggest sour cherry orchard in the world, and also the home of the Cherry Home Canning Company, a firm which owns its own lake steamer and cans its own cherries.

Rolling over hill after hill the Cherry Home orchards cover scores of acres and at the same time are surrounded by other orchards privately owned. This orchard probably represents the biggest cherry unit in the world.

When the cherry season rolls around and the harvest is nearly ready, school girls in parties of from ten upward, each in the care of chaperone, start arriving at the orchard to aid in the harvest. For a month or more these hundred or more girls live a semi-military life, picking cherries during the day time, having their summer play in the later afternoon and evening, and spending their nights in the modern dormitories provided for them.

As soon as the cherries are harvested they are hauled directly to the canning plant and a short time after they have left the trees they are steaming in the cans, ready to make cherry pies for the whole world.

— Traverse City Record Eagle, July 30, 1926

Camp Caho

Camp Caho was a summer camp for girls operated at
Cherry Home from 1916 through the early 1930s. The
camp consisted of sleeping lodges along the shore, a dining
hall, a craft building, a main lodge, and riding stables.
Outdoor activities included swimming, canoeing, horseback
riding, tennis, golf, target practice, and hiking. The girls received arts
and crafts and nature lessons. They were also offered automobile
driving lessons in the camp's Ford motor cars.

Cat's-head Point Lighthouse

Cat's-head Light — *Cat's-head Point on which
is located Cat's-head Lighthouse, is by road about nine
miles from Northport, and is ever an object of interest
to visitors, although its lighthouse does not offer the
picturesque features so often possessed by these beacons
of dangerous shores, being simply a strong, commodious
dwelling for the keeper and his family, having a small
tower in which is kept, in the immaculate spotlessness ever
required by Uncle Sam, the great revolving globe of light
that safeguards that approach to Grand Traverse Bay.*

— *Sprague's History of Grand Traverse
and Leelanau Counties,* 1903

Indians Will Have Fair

An event of much interest to the people of the county and especially to the summer people is the Indian fair that will be held at the Indian camp grounds two miles south of Northport, Thursday, Friday and Saturday, August 19, 20 and 21.

This is under the direction of George Pontiac, an Indian who is a descendent of Chief Pontiac, and who has made extensive study of the traditions and old customs of his race. Assisted by Jonas Shawn-da-se and others he will give demonstrations of war dances, telling the purpose of the dances and explaining many other things about the red man of which the whites are ignorant. Demonstrations will be given of basket making, canoe making, and descriptions of how hides were tanned.

There will be two programs daily, beginning at 3:00 and 8:30 p.m. eastern standard time.

— *Leelanau Enterprise,* August 12, 1926

Indian Camp Meeting

Near Northport are the camp meeting grounds of the Indians of the Methodist faith of the Northwest. Here in August they hold their annual camp meeting services and renew tribal acquaintances. Noted speakers of national prominence address them and the services are full of deepest meaning and interest.

— *Grand Traverse, the Summer Land,* circa 1910

Omena

Omena is located about midway along Leelanau County's west shore on Grand Traverse Bay. It is situated five miles south of Northport, 11 miles northeast of Leland, and 25 miles north of Traverse City.

Omena had its beginnings in 1852 when the Reverend Peter Dougherty and a band of Ottawas and Chippewas led by Chief Ahgosa moved across the bay from the Old Mission Peninsula to establish a new settlement. Dougherty named the new settlement "New Mission," which was located on the bluffs about one mile east of the present village. O-me-nah is an Indian word meaning "is that so?" Reverend Dougherty often would use this expression, which amused the Native Americans and they suggested that the village be named Omena. Dougherty built a two-story building with lumber brought over from Old Mission, which was used as a meeting place and mission school for the Native American children. In 1858 Dougherty built the white Congregational Church that still stands today. Now called the Omena Presbyterian Church, it is one of the oldest historical landmarks in Northern Michigan. The New Mission manse was erected that same year.

Omena was the earliest resort area in Leelanau County. The first summer resort appears to have been the Shab-Wah-Sing, named after the Native American chief who had occupied New Mission Point. It was built on Omena Bay about 1868, and came to be known as the Chicago Club, as its guests were mainly from that city. In 1884 Dougherty's mission was sold to a group of Cincinnati businessmen and remodeled to become the Leelanau Hotel. Two other buildings and five summer cottages were soon added to the resort. The Leelanau Hotel was a prominent summer resort in its day and continued to operate until 1914. Neglect took its toll and the hotel was torn down in 1929.

The resort business drew Frank Graves of Grand Rapids to Omena. He purchased 159 acres of choice Omena property with plans to build a summer resort. The original Omena Inn was built about 1891-92. The resort property was platted in 1893 for summer homes and soon several cottages were constructed along the shore of the point. After only a few successful years in operation, the Omena Inn burned down in 1904.

The Clovers was built about 1898 and consisted of several buildings — the Main House, the Big Cottage, the Little Cottage, the Bay Cottage, and an employees' building. The Clovers was aptly named, for the 22 acres surrounding the hotel were covered with fragrant clover blossoms. A dining facility was built to serve 100. Besides guests at the hotel, visitors from other resorts and cottages

View from Dock, Omena, Mich.

would often take their meals at the Clovers. The guests dressed for dinner every night and were served fresh fruits, vegetables and dairy products that were produced on the Clovers' grounds. A dance band from the University of Illinois provided music for meals in the dining room and special dance parties in the social hall. The Clovers operated until the early 1950s.

The Sunset Lodge was built in 1898 and operated for about 50 years. As its popularity increased, additional buildings were added, first two cottages, then a dining room and social hall, summer kitchen, and a barn for horses and carriages. A garden provided fresh fruits and vegetables for the summer guests. The Sunset Lodge offered tennis courts and lawn croquet. Entertainment in the form of picnics, hayrides, charades, and dancing were offered. The favorable summer climate brought more and more visitors to the area, and some returned to build summer cottages. The Oaks was originally built as a summer cottage, but was converted to a hotel about 1900. It operated for about 20 years under various owners and managers. The Oaks' gracious veranda was a favorite spot for its guests. It burned down in 1938.

The second Omena Inn opened in 1920 in the remodeled New Mission manse. Wings were added to accommodate more summer visitors. It operated on and off for a number of years under different owners.

About 1908 a two-story pavilion was built at Omena Point, close to the shore. The pavilion served as the social center of the summer colony. Amateur theatre shows, carnivals, and weekly dances with live orchestras were popular activities with the resorters. In 1952 the Omena-Traverse Yacht Club took over the building.

The docks at Omena were busy all summer with passenger steamers bringing summer visitors to the area. The Traverse Bay Line of steamers made three stops a day so guests could make connections with Traverse City. Railroad service came to Omena in 1903 when the Traverse City, Leelanau and Manistique Railroad was completed from Traverse City to Northport. The train brought more visitors daily to the busy resort area. Omena had two stops, one at the Clovers, and the other at the village.

Omena village catered to the summer tourists as well as the local farmers. By 1900 Omena had a general store, two real estate agents, three carpenters, a mason, a blacksmith, two teachers, a milliner, a surveyor, and a flourmill, as well as the several resorts already mentioned.

With the changing tastes of the motoring public, the old resorts gradually declined and vanished. The leisurely resort vacation gave way to faster travel and shorter stays. But some of the old Omena resort atmosphere still survives in the many beautiful summer homes and the families that have kept the cottage colony alive and well.

Omena — *a picturesque and interesting Indian village. The village lies in a pretty cove close to the shore. Above rises a high bluff upon which is situated the large Leelanaw Hotel with beautiful grounds and affording magnificent views. The history of Omena is closely connected with that of Old Mission, across the west arm of the bay. In connection with the missionary and educational work organized at Old Mission, a station was established here in 1852. This philanthropy was conducted by the Presbyterian Church as one of its mission enterprises for many years. The old church still remains in the center of the quaint little village...*

— Inglis, *Northern Michigan, Handbook for Travelers,* 1898

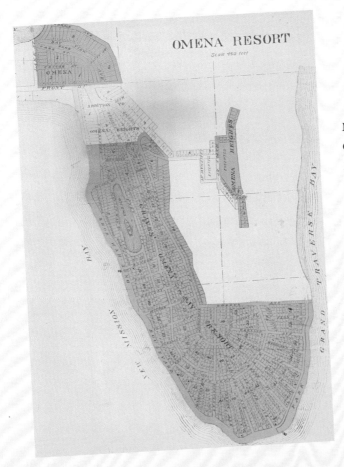

Map of Omena Resort, *Atlas of Leelanau County,* 1900
Omena is located on the west shore of Grand Traverse Bay, 11 miles northeast of Leland, and 25 miles north of Traverse City. In 1900 Omena's population was 300, but swelled to 800 in the summer. During the navigational season there was daily connection by steamer with Traverse City and Northport. Omena supported a Congregational and a Presbyterian church. It had a general store, two boarding houses, three hotels and a summer resort, two real estate agents, three carpenters, a mason, a painter, a blacksmith, two teachers, a milliner, a surveyor, a fisherman, and a flourmill.

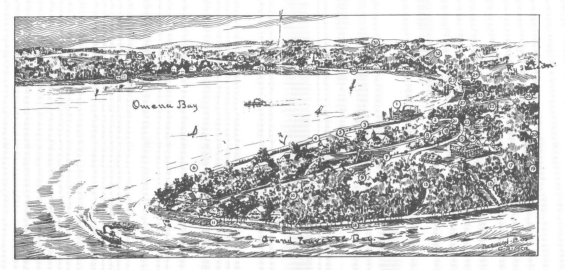

Guide to Omena Resort Grounds.

1—Omena Resort Dock.
2—Road to Leelanaw Hotel.
3 Beach Road to Omena Inn.
4—Sidewalk to Omena Inn.
5—Rustic Stairs leading to Indian Garden. Picnic Ground .
6—Omena Inn, on extreme southern point of resort grounds.
7—Leelanaw Avenue, through orchard'.
8—Woods road from North end of grounds to Omena Inn.
9—Orchard of 5000 trees.
10—Heart's Ease, under the Wild Grape Arbor.
11—Boulevard drive from Omena Inn, to Leelanaw Hotel.
12—Happy Hunting Ground remains of Indians .

13—Lovers' Lane. Don't miss it.
14—Leelanaw Hotel The view is one of surpassing beauty.
15—Lookout from Tower of Leelanaw Hotel: on a clear day can see 20 miles
16—Stairs in front of Leelanaw Hotel, descending a terrace of 150 feet.
17—Winding Stairs to Mineral Spring below.
18—Farm and Garden Supplies.
19—Singing Sands and Bathing Ground .
20—Engall's Bay
21—Rustic Summer House, overlooking Bay and Omena Village.
22—Avenue of Walnut trees, to Leelanaw Hotel
23—Macadamized Road through Omena Village.

24—Omena Village.
25—Indian Church and Cemetery of many years ago.
26—Beautiful drive to Northport, Cat Head Point and Light House.
27—Road from Omena Village to Leland.
28—Road from Omena Village to Indian Village. Fine Scenery.
21—Manseau's Trout Pond, about 3 miles South from Village.
30—Indian Burying Ground, near Indian Village.
31—Carp Lake, 7 miles west.
32—Bass Lake, 2 miles west.
33—Old Chicago Club House, first house in Omena.
For livery rigs and boat livery, inquire at Hotels.
Telegraph and Post Office at Omena Village.

For Resort Book, Plat of Grounds, Rent of Cottages, etc., inquire of ABEL T. PAGE, Special Agent, Grand Rapids, Mich., or the owner, F. H. GRAVES, Grand Rapids, Mich. Omena during the season.

— Omena Resort, circa 1898

Similar to the majority of the resorts in this region, Omena Resort is built up in the midst of the virgin forest; and the roads and drives which circle in and out of the deep cool woods are particularly picturesque and rugged and well suited for bicycling and driving. The resort is situated upon a commanding piece of ground, considerably above the surface of the lake, giving an excellent view of the surrounding country. Here about six hundred acres of well-shaded, grassy land, dotted with picturesque and often elegant cottages, and two large hotels, constitute the resort...

Fruit and vegetables are easily obtainable in the neighborhood; the water supply is from flowing wells and water from the bay. With the excellent hotels and the numerous cottages, the attractiveness of this resort, practically new, has increased the population from about four hundred in the winter to something in the neighborhood of fifteen hundred during the summer months.

— Michigan: A Summer and Health Resort State, 1898

185

Omena, The Beautiful, is located about mid-way and upon the west shore of Grand Traverse Bay. Here, nature has bestowed her most lavish gifts of loveliness and beauty upon woodland and waters; She has molded the rolling hills, clad them in the most enticing forests, and washed the foothills with the sparkling crystal waters of Omena Bay, where storms seldom disturb it, and the tiny little pleasure boats can ride in safety. There are no marshes or stagnant water to be found here, objects can be plainly seen where the water is from twenty to thirty feet in depth. The pure and bracing atmosphere has a magic and beneficial effect upon the people so unfortunate as to be afflicted with malaria or hay fever. The summer tourists begin to flock here from every quarter of the United States and many have become so fascinated with the loveliness of the place that they have built beautiful homes. The accommodations for the summer tourist are ample and of the best, The Leelanaw, The Omena Inn, The Clovers, Cheminwhay and The Sunset Lodge, are all well designed for the comfort and pleasure of the guests and the best recommend we hear for them is that those who come once, come again.

— Beauty Spots in Leelanau, 1901 Souvenir

No other state in the union is so richly endowed with romantic nature as Michigan, and no other region is so abundant in those gifts as Omena Resort.

Omena is 20 miles north of Traverse City, down the west arm of Grand Traverse Bay, and is accessible by the lake line steamers and by the bay steamers which connect with the G.R. & I. and C. & W. M. Railroads at Traverse City, making several trips daily, and affording tired and dusty passengers a delightful and refreshing two hours ride into the most picturesque region of America. Omena Resort receives two mails each day and maintains a telegraph and express facilities.

— Omena Resort, circa 1903

Omena is an important resort located at Omena Point on Grand Traverse Bay, twenty miles north of Traverse City. The point extends about a mile into the bay and is heavily wooded, the land lies high and is a beautiful spot in every way. It can be reached by railroad, the station being the town of Omena, which is a mile and a half from the Point …

The roads around it are good and the woods have retained their natural beauty. Picnic grounds, play grounds, etc., have been made, and considerable rustic work in the form of bridges and pavilions, etc. has been made.

— Michigan in Summer, 1904

RUSTIC ARCH, OMENA, MICH.

A line with fish

With all the fishing, the finny population in these waters will never be diminished. The whole country contiguous to Omena Resort abounds in small lakes, and cold trout and bass streams, while the bay furnishes ample sport for those who prefer to cast their hooks for the festive deep water Mackinaw trout and other varieties. A fishing expedition here means large success and no failures. Livery rigs may be engaged at the Omena Inn.

— *Omena Resort*, circa 1901

Hotel Leelanau

We do not know of a more desirable family home for summer any-
where than "The Leelanau" at Omena. Located in the north half of
the peninsula, it insures an air so pure and an entire summer so free
from heat, malaria, mosquitos and insects, that the average pleasure
seeker or invalid must here find the rest or cure desired. Omena is
one of the most desirable places in the country for persons afflicted
with hay fever, the atmosphere affording immediate relief.

— *The Leelanau, Omena, Michigan, Season of 1900*

Hotel Leelanau, Omena, Mich.

Hotel Leelanau, Omena, Traverse Bay, Mich.

Omena Heights, Michigan

This fine little peninsula, almost an island, seems to have been designed by
nature for a place of rest. Rising by gentle slopes and undulations from the
pebbly beach to a height of some 150 feet above the level of the bay, it
commands a view of the lake, bay, and surrounding country for many miles.
At the summit of this height in a beautiful and picturesque spot is situated
"The Leelanau," a quiet, homelike place, constructed in a substantial manner,
with comfortable, well-finished and plastered rooms, with a large dining
room, ladies' parlor, gents' sitting room, wide porches and all necessary
attachments to render it a most desirable family home for the summer;
also a large annex, affording elegant, quiet rooms for families.

— *The Leelanau, Omena, Michigan, Season of 1900*

The grounds of The Leelanau Hotel are large, and numerous shade trees (maple, elm, etc.) have been left where nature placed them. The dense forests are here as they appeared to the pioneer of 100 years ago, and even the aborigines of these beautiful forests, or a remnant of them, are to be found at an Indian village not far from Omena Heights.

This property is owned by an association of business men in Cincinnati, many of whom have private cottages on the grounds, which embrace about six hundred acres of land. A portion of the tract is under cultivation and supplies the hotel with an abundance of vegetables and the choicest fruits in their season. The orchard is the largest in northern Michigan, containing 4,000 bearing fruit trees.

— *The Leelanau, Omena, Michigan, Season of 1900*

VIEW FROM HOTEL LEELANAU OMENA, MICH.

Cottage at Omena Resort, Mich.

People from all points of the East and South are flocking to Omena resort to build their summer houses, impelled by the faultless climate and the grandeur of the spot; and though there is a large demand for building lots, prices have not as yet advanced. Excellent lots, averaging 50 x 125 feet, with shade and water view may now be had at prices upward from $50.00, but with many expensive improvements, recently made, the fine hotels and cottages, and the demand increasing, prices must naturally advance. Omena Resort is now recognized as Queen of all watering places in Northern Michigan, the mecca for summer tourists, and those who act promptly and take advantage of the original low prices made when the resort was platted, and before it had acquired its present perfection and magnitude, may consider themselves fortunate indeed. Lots are offered on easy terms.

— *Omena Resort*, circa 1903

Hymn to Omena.

Composed by
Miss Richmond
and
Mrs. Willard.

Omena, the gem of creation,
The home of the evergreen tree,
The shrine of the tourist's devotion
We offer our homage to thee.
May thy lovers, united, ne'er falter,
But e'er to thy forests prove true;
Omena, we're thine, now and ever—
Three cheers for thy waters so blue.

O the sail-boat, the sail-boat, "The Viking,"
With Peterson firm at the helm,
For thee we'll forsake even biking,
To roam over Neptune's broad realm.
We will mount every high, foaming billow
That rises with feathery crest,
Or we'll float o'er thy calm, gentle wavelets,
With our oars and our cares all at rest.

O "beautiful gift," fair Omena,
To the winds we thy colors unfold,
The green for thy blossoming spring-time,
For thy autumn, the crimson and gold.
We will sing of Omena the glorious,
Every year brings new joys to our view;
Omena, Omena, victorious!
Three cheers for thy waters so blue!

Chorus—

Three cheers for thy waters so blue,
Three cheers for thy waters so blue,
Omena, Omena, victorious,
Three cheers for thy waters so blue!

The Omena Yell.

Hobble gobble, razzle dazzle,
Zip, boom, bah!
Omena, Omena, rah, rah, rah!

Omena Colors.

Crimson, green and gold.

Hymn to Omena — *Omena Resort, circa 1901*

The Clovers

S.A. Keyes, Proprietor

Omena, Michigan

Beautiful view of Grand Traverse Bay

to be had from every room

Orchard of 2000 trees

Vegetables fresh from the garden

Our own Jersey dairy and poultry

We make our own butter

WEST SHORE OF BAY

BOATING and BATHING UNSURPASSED

Boat livery in connection

Rates $2.00 to $2.50

Rates by week or season

The Oaks is situated on the west side of Grand Traverse Bay, 25 miles north of Traverse City, Mich. The house stands on a point and commands a fine view of the bay. The grounds are extensive and well wooded, and afford a very pleasant place for recreation...there is good bathing and the nearby lakes provide good fishing.

...The house will accommodate 40 guests. The rooms are light and airy and the beds good. There is also a well equipped laundry. The table is noted for its good home cooking. There is a large kitchen garden in connection with the house and fresh vegetables are served throughout the season. There is plenty of certified milk, cream, butter and eggs, and fresh fish from the cool deep waters of the bay. The table is of that generous, wholesome nature that builds one up after a strenuous winter in the city. The drinking water is excellent and has been pronounced "O K" by our State Board of Health.

The aim of the management is to give guests a real taste of the simple and beautiful life of the country. It is just the place to wear comfortable or sport clothes; the place to bring your family and friends; a place to enjoy hiking, fishing, swimming, and all the pleasures of the great out-of-doors.

The weather is usually cool and delightful — the nights always cool enough to make blankets a necessity. The air is wonderfully clear and bracing. Those suffering from hay-fever find relief.

Rates are $3.00 a day; $14.00 to $21.00 a week for adults; children under 5 years of age, half price.

— "The Oaks," 1922

Sunset Lodge, Omena, Mich.

Sunset Lodge Overlooks Bay

And It Has Held Its Vantage Point Since the Summer of '98

Sunset Lodge has overlooked Grand Traverse Bay from a bluff within Omena village since 1898 and is in operation for its 28th consecutive season now under the management of C.E. Wheeler.

Here is located a group of modern buildings overlooking a bay so beautiful that it has been rated as one of the five most picturesque bays in the United States. Omena is an Indian word meaning "beautiful" and has been rightly used. It is one of the pioneer resort districts of Northern Michigan, having attracted vacationists when the pine was still uncut. Through the years with additions, improvements and better facilities for handling resort trade, Omena has become one of the leading resorts of the region.

Sunset Lodge has played a great part in opening up of Leelanau summerland. To those seeking change, recreation, and healthful diversions in their summer vacations, the location of this resort offers some distinctive advantages. It is situated on the west shore of Grand Traverse Bay, twenty miles north of Traverse City…The climatic influence of the surrounding bodies of water, Grand Traverse Bay and Lake Michigan, insures an atmosphere refreshing and bracing.

— Traverse City Record Eagle, June 27, 1928

Advertisement — Sunset Lodge

— Traverse City Record Eagle, 1936

View from Summer House, Sunset Lodge, Omena, Mich.

Hello Seth,

How do you like your new position?

I thank you for the card. This is our spooning

place. How do you like it? It is a dear old place.

— Your friend, Eliz.

Postmarked Omena, 1909

Mailed to Manistee, Michigan

AM TAKING SOME FINE STROLLS AT OMENA, MICH.

The Tonic Air of Omena

It is well established truth that to the invalid or person of delicate
health, a change of climate and scenery, pure air and sunshine will
result beneficially when doctors and medicines fail. To all those who
want exclusiveness without loneliness, refreshing rest for the brain,
the nerves and the body, and an air tonic, which at once restores the
asthmatic or hay fever patient to perfect health, we recommend
Omena with a positive assurance of the desired results. The climate
here is anti-malaria, anti-depression and full of that inspiring
wine of life which cheers and stimulates.

— *Omena Resort, circa 1903*

Rebecca Richmond's
cottage at Omena, circa 1900

Thurs. August 18, 1910

Cool and breezy. Andrew and I have enlarged the seating capacity of the sky-parlor, two benches and built a platform and table, the last covered with birch bark. Mrs. Howard and Ellen, Delia Hazletine and Josephine MacBride spent the afternoon there in hammocks.

— From the unpublished diaries of Rebecca Richmond, 1910

Anderson's Store is Over Half Century Mark of Business

Trading has been carried on for 53 years in the store building occupied by Anderson's General Store at Omena. Back in early days of the region much of the patronage was furnished by the Indians. Many an old settler in the locality can recount tales of a half century ago that would leave the average listener spellbound. Since the Indians' time it has been the farmers largely who supported the store. In the past few years, however, summer tourists have become such an asset to the business that everything is being done to encourage them to make Omena their headquarters while in the north country.

— *Traverse City Record Eagle,* June 30, 1935

Omena Inn Has a Great Setting

*No artist with brush or pen could paint a picture to justify the
lovely surroundings of Omena Inn, a favorite summer vacation
spot on M-22 between Suttons Bay and Northport. For ten years
Mrs. Tom Cordoray has been hostess at the Inn. Every detail for
the assurance of guest comfort and pleasure is under her direct
supervision. These details are so painstakingly worked out that
select tourists from distant localities make it their summer home
without thought of going elsewhere.*

*Every building comprising the resort is a model in cleanli-
ness and comfort. The main building is a spacious white frame
structure with a screened-in front porch which offers an excellent
view overlooking beautiful Omena Bay. Inside the Inn are rooms
that possess homelike qualities seldom found in summer hotels.
There is a large sitting room, lounge, recreation room and private dining room. The main dining room, located on the
southern side of the building, is tastefully done in blue and white, with each table
sporting snowy linen and shiny service. The kitchen, from whence come chicken and steak dinners famous for their high
quality, is clean to a minute degree. The second floor of the structure is given over to guest rooms furnished in taste. This
feature is especially noticeable throughout the Inn. Every room has running water with bath. Expensive furniture,
pictures, tapestries and excellent interior decoration lend distinct class to Omena Inn.*

— Traverse City Record Eagle, June 30, 1935

Omena Village. Like a picture in Switzerland it nestles close
to the foot hills of Omena Resort, where every want of the
cottager is supplied from the village stores. Fresh milk, fruits,
vegetables, meats and ice are delivered daily at the cottages,
and garbage is removed each morning.

— Omena Resort, circa 1903

Solle's Bookshop

Solle's Bookshop…is a swanky bit of Old New York in a
rural setting — and what a setting on the shore of Omena
Bay. The sun was shining on the blue water, and the
rushes were bending beneath the breeze, and the shop's
picture window making a frame of it all. The door that
you open into the shop just looks like any other door, but
it isn't. It's a door leading to a magical world — the
world of books…To us, this bookshop is one of Leelanau's
greatest possessions. Through its portals, one may - not
only reach for the stars — but touch them.

— *Leelanau Enterprise*, August 10, 1939

ADVERTISEMENT — SOLLE'S BOOKSHOP
— *Resort Directory of Leland*, 1937

Suttons Bay

Suttons Bay is situated on Grand Traverse Bay, three and one-half miles from the geographical center of Leelanau County, 16 miles north of Traverse City and 12 miles south of Northport.

In 1865 Harry C. Sutton platted an area which comprised three or four city blocks, now included in the southern end of the village. The Register of Deeds recorded the settlement as Suttonsburg. It was a modest beginning, but Father Andrew Herbstrit had bigger plans for the village. In 1871 he platted hundreds of lots and changed the name to Pleasantville, but later referred to it as Pleasant City. Father Herbstrit had plans to establish a Catholic university and convent, but his dream never materialized. With time and local usage, the village became known as Suttons Bay.

Like other lakeshore communities, Suttons Bay's first industry was cutting cordwood for steamships. The lumber industry soon followed. At the height of the lumbering era, Suttons Bay had four sawmills and six docks. As lumbering declined, cherry farming and tourism became the prominent industries. Several of the passenger steamers made Suttons Bay a port of call including the *Missouri*, *Illinois*, and *Kansas* of the Northern Michigan line and the *Columbia*, *Crescent*, and *Lou A. Cummings* of the Traverse Bay Line.

For a small village Suttons Bay was well equipped with hotel accommodations for its early visitors. The Union House was built in 1871 and the Bay House in 1874. The Seiber House was built as a saloon, but later was converted to a hotel. The Park Hotel with its double-decked veranda was built in 1890. It was an elegant hotel for its day and catered to traveling salesmen. It provided livery service and had a sample room for salesmen to show their wares. The Park Hotel was a popular landmark in the village until it burned in 1915.

When the Traverse City, Leelanau and Manistique Railroad went through from Traverse City to Northport in 1903, Suttons Bay became a regular stop. A boxcar was

Wonderful weather. Everyone feeling fine. Russell and I are just ready to start for Fountain Point for a day's fishing. R. lost four or five lbs. mack trout out in front of the cottage this morn. because he didn't have landing net with him.

— Luella —

Postmarked Suttons Bay, 1919
Mailed to Auburn, New York

used for a station until a fine stone depot was built in 1920. The railroad brought changes to the community. The stagecoach routes were eliminated, and the Traverse Bay Line of steamers stopped running. Mail and freight arrived daily. People no longer needed to stockpile goods for the winter. Business prospered. Suttons Bay has long had a thriving business district. An 1880 description of the village reads:

"Suttons Bay is a lively place of 250 or 300 inhabitants, containing four stores, two hotels, a fine brick schoolhouse, a sawmill, printing office, blacksmith and shoe shops etc. Quite an extensive mercantile business is transacted at this place, and being situated in the center of a tract of valuable farm land, it must inevitably become a village of importance."[1]

Suttons Bay did indeed become a village of importance, supplying a large part of Leelanau County with goods and services. Cottages were built along the shore and a tourist camp just north of town was established about 1926. Suttons Bay never was predominantly a resort community, but established itself as the center of commerce for the area.

[1] Traverse region, Historical and Descriptive. Chicago: H.R. Page & Co., 1884, page 247

Sutton's Bay is a prosperous little community, having many natural advantages as a summer resort — good hotels, good liveries and is a mecca for fishermen. This thriving little town has a permanent population of about six hundred, and is located about seventeen miles north of Traverse City, on the T.C.L. & M. R'y, reached by the Grand Rapids and Indiana resort trains to Traverse City. There is an interesting flowing well, with head enough to carry the water up a hillside to a reservoir which supplies the town with water for all purposes. The Park Hotel and Sutton's Bay Hotel furnish good accommodations.

— Michigan in Summer, 1910

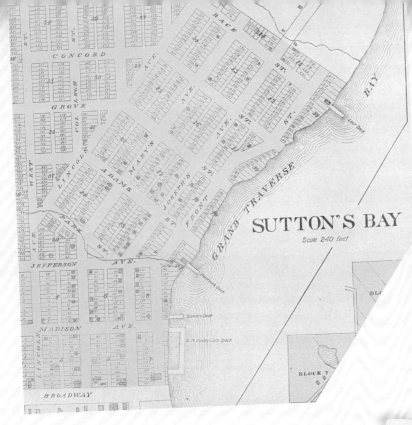

MAP OF SUTTONS BAY, *Atlas of Leelanau County*, 1900
Suttons Bay, located nine miles southeast of Leland,
had a population of 600 in 1900. It had daily stage
service to Traverse City, which was the nearest railroad
point until 1903. Suttons Bay had three hotels, two
liveries, three saloons, two masons, two shoemakers,
two general stores, a lawyer, a physician, a druggist,
and an undertaker.

Larson's Park Hotel
Claus Warner, Proprietor,
Suttons Bay, Mich.

This house is so located that guests can overlook the beautiful
waters of Grand Traverse Bay and in the midst of fine trout
streams and just a few rods from the depot. It is furnished with
hot and cold water, bath rooms and steam heat. Also has an
elegant sample room in connection.

We have a good livery for the accommodation of the
traveling public. Call and see us and you will go away happy.

Rates are $1.00 to $2.00 per day. Special rates by the week.

— Advertisement from *Leelanau Enterprise*, July 13, 1903

Park Hotel
Suttons Bay, Mich.

Suttons Bay

Suttons Bay, at the head of the bay whence its name, offers many attractions to the summer visitor. The roads are excellent, the fishing of the finest, and boating, bathing and the usual summer sports serve to pleasantly fill the time of the visitor in search of rest and healthful recreation.

The Park Hotel is conveniently located and gives good accommodations and service. The liveries are equipped to provide carriages and horses for riding or driving. Lake Leelanau, only four miles west over good roads, is the most noted fishing grounds of the northwest.

— *Grand Traverse, the Summer Land*, 1910

Suttons Bay
Leelanau County's Trading Center

Suttons Bay merchants can supply the summer visitors with the highest grade groceries; smartest most up-to-date clothing and shoes, gas, oil and tires; a modern barber shop; baking services; drugs, confectionery and gifts. The Suttons Bay merchants have chosen merchandise of the kind that the resorter desires. Suttons Bay stores are noted for their low prices on quality merchandise. "We don't try to Jesse James the Resorter." We want them to come back.

— *Traverse City Record Eagle*, June 29, 1929

2 - St. Joseph Ave., Suttons Bay, Mich.

St. Joseph Avenue

Suttons Bay
Where Life's Worth Living

You will not make any mistakes on your Pike tour if you make a stop of at least an hour or two in the beautiful and modern village of Suttons Bay. Situated on the shores of the beautiful, sparkling sheet of water for which the town is named, there is always a delightfully cool breeze blowing from the Bay even on the hottest of summer days, making Suttons Bay an ideal place to make a stop on the long ride.

Suttons Bay has two good hotels — the Park Place and the Suttons Bay Hotel — both with all modern conveniences, situated with a good view of the Bay, furnished with the best of rooms, and supplied with all the means of serving meals par excellence. If your stay in the village is to be a short one, your needs of light lunch materials, ice cream, cooling drinks, etc., can be supplied by restaurant and soda fountain.

Mr. Smiseth and Mr. Thorson, respective proprietors of our two garages, are well prepared to do with neatness and dispatch any repair work that may be needed. You are sure to receive courteous treatment and quick work from either of these men, should your needs be in this direction. Both garages are equipped with a gasoline filling station, as also are the stores of L.R. Sogge and Messrs. Husby, Hanson & Co., so that the life fluid of your motor is easily obtainable here.

Welcome to Suttons Bay, where life's worth living.

— West Michigan Pike, 1914

The Traverse City, Leelanau and Manistique Railroad reached Suttons Bay in 1903. The train service operated out of a boxcar until the depot was built in 1920. Note the "Railroad Crossing" sign which was placed quite high to be visible above the winter snowfall.

Suttons Bay, Mich.

Suttons Bay Most Hospitable

One of the most progressive villages of Michigan is Suttons Bay, located 18 miles north of Traverse City on M-22. It has become the supply center for a large section of the Leelanau county resort region and the summer visitors find its merchants courteous and accommodating in the extreme.

Suttons Bay maintains a fine tourist camp just north of the village and has come to be known as one of the best-kept municipal camps in Northern Michigan. It lies away from the dust of the highway and although adjacent to the road, it is hidden from traffic. The bay shore is nearby.

— Traverse City Record Eagle, July 27, 1927

Livliest Community

Suttons Bay calls itself the "Liveliest Community in Leelanau County." It has all the facilities for an ideal vacation spot as well as a thriving business community …Suttons Bay is noted for its well-kept homes and its community spirit. Summer visitors always find a friendly welcome in the pleasant village.

— "Vacation Handbook and Fisherman's Guide, Leelanau County," *Leelanau Enterprise,* 1942

Tea Room, Suttons Bay

This rustic tea room was operated by Nellie Bahle in the mid 1920s. It was located on the east side of St. Joseph Street.

Dear Aunt Mary,

Another of my dreams has come true. Dan, his girl friend and I are on a five day auto trip along the lake in Michigan. We stop when we get tired and have had a cottage both nights by a different lake. It is fun not to have a destination.

— Grace

Postmark not legible, 1932
Mailed to Alcott, New York

Dear All —

Slept in a cabin at Big Rapids, ate breakfast there and left at 7:30. Arrived in Traverse City at about 9:30. Went to Gardner's store. (Aphra's Mother and Dad) Talked to them until about 10 o'clock & arrived in Sutton's Bay shortly. Have a nice log cabin. John & Arnie went fishing last night. You should see how BIG they were. Had them for breakfast this A/M. Going to Methodist Church today.

Postmark and date not legible
Mailed to Zeeland, Michigan

ADVERTISEMENT
— "Vacation Handbook and Fisherman's Guide, Leelanau County,"
Leelanau Enterprise, 1938

The Hermit

Rock Tybushwsky (spellings vary) was a local character of fame known as "the Hermit." He was of Polish origin and moved to the region from Posen, Michigan. It was said that he studied for the priesthood, but gave it up to become a teacher. He could speak 13 languages. Rock made his first home about 1900 in a hillside dugout near the railroad tracks on M-22. Later he settled in a sod hut just north of Belanger Pond on the same road. He survived by growing his own vegetables, keeping chickens and some livestock. His cattle would often accompany him on his trips into Suttons Bay. What he was not able to raise for himself, he managed to do without. Occasionally neighbors and passersby would give him small donations. With a heavy beard and tattered clothes, the Hermit presented a curious spectacle to tourists and photographers. He lived to be about 84 years of age and died at the Traverse City State Asylum.

North & South Manitou Islands

North Manitou Island

North Manitou Island is about seven miles long and four miles wide, and covers about 15,000 acres. It is located 12 miles west of Leland.

Timber played a big role in the history of North Manitou Island. In 1846 Nicholas and Simon Pickard established a wooding station. It supplied steamers traveling through the Manitou Passage with cordwood, fish, and fresh produce. Pickard built wooding docks at several places on the island. Logging became more extensive in the 1850s. Sawmills were built and milled lumber was shipped to Chicago.

The vast tracts of land that had been cleared of timber drew farmers to the island. The first home-stead claim was filed in 1875. Later, other enterprises followed, including Silas Boardman's livestock farm and Frederic Beuham's fruit orchards. Boardman later sold his farm to Franklin Newhall and his son, Benjamin, who developed extensive fruit orchards, including apples, pears, plums, apricots, and cherries. The Newhalls also promoted the island as a resort and took in summer visitors.

With increasing vessel traffic traveling past North Manitou Island, there was a need to help ships in distress. Beginning in 1854, a volunteer lifesaving crew operated out of a government approved boat-house, which was constructed on the east side of the island. Twenty years later the U.S. Life-Saving Service was established. A lifeboat station was built in 1877 and a paid keeper was hired with a volunteer crew. A year later a regularly enlisted crew of six men was hired. In 1887 separate living quarters for the crew were built.

On the southern point of the island a lighthouse keeper's dwelling and foghorn building were erected in 1897. A wooden light tower was built the following year. It was abandoned in 1935 and later destroyed by a severe storm and pulled into Lake Michigan. The dangerous shoals offshore necessitated a second safety measure. From 1910 to 1935 a lightship was anchored on the shoals to mark the treach-erous passage. It was replaced with a permanent structure officially known as the North Manitou Shoal Light, but locally known as "the Crib," which rises to a height of 75 feet above the water and still flashes its warning light today.

In the 1890s a group of friends from Chicago, including Silas Boardman's married daughter, Carrie Blossom, built the first summer cottages on the island. The resort colony came to be known as "Cottage Row." These resorters came north from Chicago on the passenger steamers, bringing with

them used building materials, including doors and windows from the Columbian Exposition of 1893, which were used in several cottages. The cottages were connected by a boardwalk and illuminated with oil lamps that led to a small hotel on the north end, run by the Newhalls, which served as a communal dining room. Later Kate Shepard took over the communal meals in her small hotel at the south end of the boardwalk. The summer population grew to 100 people, all of whom took their meals at the Shepard hotel. The only transportation between the islands and the mainland in the early days was by the mail boat. In 1913 the Grosvenor family established regular ferry and mail service between Leland and North Manitou Island.

Meanwhile on the other side of the island the lumbering business boomed when in 1908 the Smith and Hull Lumber Company of Traverse City built a sawmill at Crescent, and constructed eight miles of railroad track to transport timber. At the height of the lumbering era, Crescent had a population of 300, a hotel, general store, post office, saloon, and school. When the sawmill stopped operations in 1917, Crescent soon became a ghost town.

The fortune of the island took another turn when in 1922 a syndicate of Chicago businessmen set out to acquire the entire island for a private hunting reserve. As part of this syndicate, William R. Angell of Continental Motors bought his first property on the island in 1926. By 1942 Angell owned 70% of the island, becoming the greatest single landowner of the island's acreage. After his death in 1950, the Angell Foundation through the Manitou Island Association managed the business operations of the island, which included lumbering, farming, cherry orchards, and breeding deer. The association sponsored annual deer hunts in November and December, when many sportsmen from the Midwest spent several days at the lodge on the island. For several years the association guaranteed that each hunter would get at least one deer to bring home.

In 1984 the Angell Foundation sold its property to the National Park Service to become part of the Sleeping Bear Dunes National Lakeshore. North Manitou Island is accessible to visitors for hiking, backpacking, and primitive camping. Exploration of historic sites includes Cottage Row, old farmsteads, and the U.S. Life-Saving Service complex, which was awarded National Historic Landmark designation in 1998.

Above: *Logging Crew from Shingleton Camp on North Manitou Island*

Advertisement — North Manitou Island Route

Leelanau Enterprise, 1909

Manitou Island's Route — Mail Boat

208

MAP OF NORTH MANITOU ISLAND, *Atlas of Leelanau County*, 1900
North Manitou Island is located off the western shore of Leelanau
County, 12 miles west of Leland. In 1900 it had a population of 150.
Steamers made stops twice a week during the navigation season, and
mail was delivered three times a week. The village of Crescent was
located on the west side of the island. In 1900 the island had a
sawmill, a lumber dealer, several fruit growers, a general store, a
hotel, a livestock rancher, a physician, and a summer resort colony.

*Lifesaving Station,
North Manitou*

The first volunteer lifesaving crew on North Manitou
Island operated out of a government supplied boat-
house in 1854. Twenty years later the U.S. Life-Saving
Service was established on the island. A lifeboat station was built in 1877 and a paid keeper was hired
with a volunteer crew. A year later a regularly enlisted
crew of six men were hired. This view of the Life-
Saving Station is from about 1910.

North Manitou, U.S. Life-Saving Service Boat and Crew

The North Manitou Life-Saving Station keeper and crew practiced launching their surfboat. This was part of their weekly regimen of duties. The routine was the same for every station throughout the Service. On Mondays the crew would drill and practice with the beach apparatus, check the boats and perform any necessary maintenance. On Tuesdays they would practice with the boats. Wednesdays would be for practicing the International Code of Signals. On Thursdays the crew would run the beach apparatus drill. On Fridays they would practice first aid on the apparently drowned. And Saturdays would be used for housekeeping.

Below: This postcard from about 1910 shows the North Manitou Island dock and the U.S. Life-Saving Service compound. On the ridge behind the Life-Saving Service buildings is the cottage colony known as "Cottage Row." As lumbering declined on the western side of the island, the growth of farming on the eastern side took hold. This eastern settlement became the hub of social and economic activity on the island.

Keeper's Dwelling

In 1897 a lighthouse keeper's dwelling and foghorn building were erected on the southern-most point of North Manitou Island. A wooden light tower was built the following year.

No. MANITOU ID. LIGHT

North Manitou Light

The North Manitou Island Lighthouse was constructed in 1898. The wooden structure was abandoned in 1935, and became a victim of shoreline erosion. A severe storm in 1941 destroyed the light-house and it was pulled into Lake Michigan.

North Manitou Island

The U.S. Post Office near the Stormer dock on the east side of North Manitou Island, circa 1910.

Twelve miles "off" shore is the North Manitou Island, which is one-half the size of a standard township. There are two villages upon the island, North Manitou, which is a summer resort and Crescent, a lumbering town, with a saw mill, railroad, boarding house, company's store, church and school. At North Manitou is a United States life-saving station. At the south end of the island is a government light, which during the hours of darkness, helps the boats to keep their bearings while passing through between the island and the mainland. Much of the island is still in its natural state and offers excellent opportunities to those who desire the excitement of exploration. The island is reached by launch from Leland.

— *Grand Traverse Region*, circa 1914

Apple Harvest
waiting for shipment to mainland

Lumbering and farming were the two primary means of livelihood on the island. Much of North Manitou's western forests of beech, hemlock, and maple trees were cut by logging crews. Lumbering on the island reached its peak about 1910. The cutover lands were attractive to farmers because the climate of the island was found to be suitable for fruit farming. Apples and cherries were the primary crops and shipping was done on steamers.

Native American Loggers

In the early 1900s lumbering brought an ethnically diverse population to North Manitou Island. Immigrants from several countries, including about 200 Russians, worked together in the logging camps. Native Americans like these four men left their homes on the mainland to join the logging crews.

Smith and Hull General Store

The Smith and Hull Company ran the lumber operations on the west side of North Manitou Island. They also ran a general store in Crescent that supplied islanders with such necessities as food, tobacco, liquor and postcards. Circa 1910.

"Manitou" Baseball Team

The North Manitou Island baseball team, circa 1910. Baseball games offered a welcome entertainment break for the islanders. Islanders had two teams that played against each other. Opposing teams sometimes traveled from the mainland to play. By 1910 the majority of the island's population was involved in logging and lived in Crescent on the west side of the island. Crescent had a dock, workers' houses, a hotel, a school, a general store, and a saloon.

Although life on the island was hard, the islanders did make time to enjoy the simple pleasures of homegrown music and watermelon.

Itinerant postcard photographer Edward Bebee, third man from the right eating watermelon, documented island life in the early 1900s.

*North Manitou
Discord Band*

A Summer Home, North Manitou

This handsome summer cottage was built in 1901 on lot #9 of Cottage Row. The Cottage Row plat was located on the ridge above the U.S. Life-Saving Service compound and all the lots had a commanding view of the Manitou Passage.

Hotel North Manitou

Located on the north end of the Cottage Row, the hotel also served as a communal dining room for the cottagers. It was later used as the Manitou Island Association lodge, until it was destroyed by fire in 1953.

Katie Shepard's Hotel

"The Beeches," which operated from 1908 to
1930, was the name of Katie Shepard's hotel on
the southern end of Cottage Row. It served as the
communal dining room after the Newhall family
discontinued meal service at the hotel on the
north end of Cottage Row.

Mr. Angell, 1944

William Angell greeted a friendly doe from the front
porch of the Monte Carlo cottage. Angell, the head
of Continental Motors from 1930 until his retire-
ment in 1939, owned 70% of the Manitou Island
Association by 1942. The Manitou Island
Association raised cattle and cherries and tried to
revive the timber business. Eventually the association's main focus became promotion of the island as
an exclusive hunting and fishing resort. For a number of years the association guaranteed that each
hunter would take home at least one deer.

Mr. Angell 1944

South Manitou Island

South Manitou is a crescent-shaped island, covering about 5,200 acres. It is three and one-half miles long and three miles wide at its widest point. It is located seven and one-half miles north of Sleeping Bear Point, and 16 miles southwest of Leland.

South Manitou Island was the site of the first European settlement in what is now Leelanau County. (Until 1894 South Manitou was part of Manitou County, as was North Manitou Island, the Fox Islands, and the Beaver Islands.) Because of the island's strategic location in the Manitou Passage and its naturally deep harbor, South Manitou was the first place of commerce in the region. The island is on the direct lake route between the straights of Mackinac and Chicago. It is the first island with a navigable harbor for ships coming from Chicago, and for southbound ships it is the last natural harbor on their way to Chicago. The naturally deep bay on its northern shore provided welcome refuge for boats in trouble, and a safe harbor in stormy weather. In 1838 the earliest recorded settlers, William Burton (Barton) and his family, settled on South Manitou Island and established a wooding station to supply passing steamers with cordwood. About this time the island was also used as a trading post for French fur-traders and Native American trappers.

The importance of South Manitou's harbor necessitated a lighthouse to help the ships navigate through the Manitou Passage. The first lighthouse, a wooden structure, was built in 1840. In 1868 a larger lighthouse keeper's dwelling was built, with a 35' tower on its roof. That lighthouse was replaced with a brick structure in 1871. This handsome structure gracefully towers 100 feet above the lake, one of the highest lighthouses on the Great Lakes.

A U.S. Life-Saving Station was established in 1902 to assist ships in distress. The station provided rescue services to ships that ran into trouble

— Sand bluffs So. Manitou Is. Mich. —

Early visitors to South Manitou must have marveled at the island's remote beauty — the high, steep bluffs, the white sandy beaches, the rich vegetation, the spectacular ancient cedar trees and the dense forests. This postcard was mailed in 1908.

as they traveled through the Manitou Passage. In 1915 the U.S. Life-Saving Service was absorbed by the U.S. Coast Guard. Both the Coast Guard and the lighthouse services on the island were closed down in 1958, leaving only the buildings standing.

The early settlers made their living by wood-cutting, farming, and tending the lighthouse and life-saving station. Three sawmills have come and gone on South Manitou, the last one operating until 1917. At one time there were six farms on the island. Because of its isolation, the island has been considered an ideal location for growing pure seed crop. Prize winning rye, beans and peas have been grown successfully on South Manitou.

Tourism supplemented the island's economy. A few summer resorts operated in the early 1900s, patronized mostly by Chicago people. Flora Haas took in summer visitors as early as 1897, followed by Mrs. Estelle Foster in 1901 and Leonard Erickson in 1907. South Manitou's early visitors must have marveled at the natural beauty of this isolated island.

Surprisingly, the Chicago fire of 1871 had an impact on South Manitou Island. Rebuilding Chicago after the fire required tons of sand and gravel. The Garden Sand Company of Chicago bought island property for the purpose of sand-mining. By the end of the century the demand for sand and gravel dwindled. With so much waterfront property on its hands, the Garden Sand Company proposed a summer resort area and platted streets and lots. (See map on page 221.) A hundred years later, we can be thankful that this plan was never brought to fruition.

Another plan to develop the island was hatched by Lee Barrett, a Detroit civic leader, who was for many years affiliated with the Eastern Michigan Resort and Tourist Association. In 1948 Barrett purchased 340 acres on the island and had plans for a "big, swanky summer hotel." Besides the hotel, Barrett planned to develop an airport and yacht anchorage, riding stables, and a nine-hole golf course. Barrett hoped that his South Manitou Island retreat would rank with Mackinac Island as one of Michigan's most exclusive, fashionable summer resorts. These elaborate plans never materialized. Only a few private cottages were built on the island.

Today, most of the island is owned by the National Park Service and is part of Sleeping Bear Dunes National Lakeshore. The former Coast Guard station now serves as a ranger's station. South Manitou is accessible to visitors for hiking, wilderness camping, and exploration of its historic sites. And like visitors from a century earlier, today's visitors still marvel at South Manitou's natural beauty.

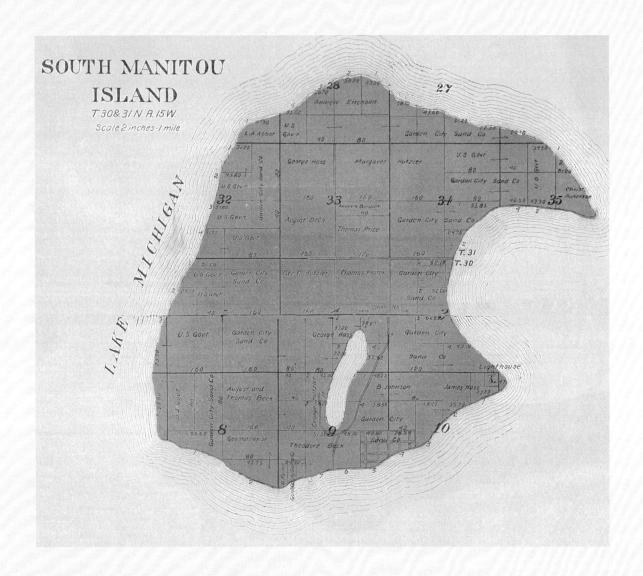

Map of South Manitou Island, *Atlas of Leelanau County,* 1900

South Manitou Island is located 16 miles southwest of Leland. In 1900 it had a population of 80 inhabitants. The island had a general store, a blacksmith, a wood dealer, several farmers, and a summer resort. The Garden City Sand Company mined sand and operated a sawmill. The plat map shows the location of various farms and the extensive holdings of the Garden City Sand Company.

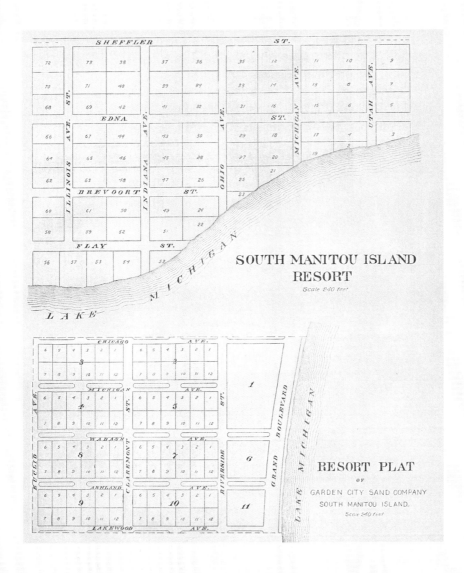

MAP OF SOUTH MANITOU ISLAND RESORT, *Atlas of Leelanau County*, 1900

This map from 1900 shows the proposed summer resort of the Garden Sand Company. Lots and streets were platted, but the resort was never developed.

South Manitou Lighthouse

The first South Manitou lighthouse and keeper's quarters were wooden structures built in 1840. They proved to be inadequate and were replaced. The keeper's house was replaced with a larger brick building in 1868. A new 100-foot brick tower was built in 1871 and an enclosed corridor was built connecting the two structures.

South Manitou-Life Saving Boat and Crew

The third U.S. Life-Saving Station along the Manitou Passage was established on South Manitou Island in 1902. The stations at North Manitou and Sleeping Bear Point were already operational. The members of the U.S. Life-Saving Service were a breed of courageous men, highly trained to assist ships in distress. Despite the danger and difficulty, the life savers invariably performed the necessary rescues.

These campers braved the remote ruggedness of South Manitou Island. It must have been quite an adventure for these young women in a time when opportunities for women were limited.

Louis Hutzler
with prize Rosen Rye, circa 1925

South Manitou Island — *Most of the land is splendidly fertile. South Manitou Island has been chosen by the Michigan State College for the supply of PURE Rosen RYE seed. Isolated as the location is, the strain remains pure and for years the rye has won first prizes at the International Hay and Grain Show in Chicago.*

— *Traverse City Record Eagle,* July 28, 1938

Other Places

Peshawbestown

Peshawbestown (various spellings) was founded in 1852 when Chief Peshaba brought a band of Ottawas from Cross Village to the western shore of the Leelanau peninsula. The Ottawas named their settlement Eagletown, but later called it Peshawbestown. By 1870 the Grand Traverse Reservation had the largest community of Native Americans in the region. The Native Americans suffered through hardship and turmoil for many years, but in 1979 federal recognition was granted to the Grand Traverse Band of Ottawa and Chippewa Indians. This paved the way to self-government and economic self-sufficiency. A sense of kinship was renewed and cultural traditions were revived. The band built a successful casino which draws many visitors to Peshawbestown.

Above: U.S. Postal Service Map of Leelanau County, 1916
This U.S. Postal Service map shows post office and postal routes in 1916. Many settlements are now ghost towns.

Right: The Peshaba family working in an orchard near Peshawbestown about 1900. From right to left are Chief Ben Peshaba, Genny Peshaba, Lucille Peshaba, and Grace Peshaba.

Women with Baskets

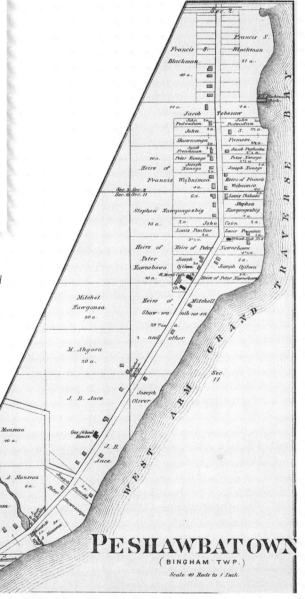

...The baskets and bead work of the Indian maidens of Ahgosa and Peshawba-town are taken as fast as they are made. Some of the finest and rarest baskets and bead work is found here, and the merchants store away great rooms full during the winter, but it fades away in the summer time like dew before the sun, so eager are the visitors to carry the Indian work back as souvenirs to their friends.

— *Beauty Spots in Leelanau*, 1901 Souvenir

MAP OF PESHAWBATOWN, *Atlas of Leelanau County*, 1881
Peshawbestown was an Ottawa settlement. This 1881 plat map shows Native American landowners.

Peshawbetown Indians

Peshawbeetown, a very interesting Indian village, is the largest of its kind in the State, which presents an interesting study of the early inhabitants of this region who have become useful citizens and self-sustaining in various pursuits.

— *Michigan in Summer,* 1910

Mary Sands, an Ottawa from the Peshawbestown area, was well-known and widely respected for her colorful birch bark and porcupine quill baskets. Ottawa artists typically used geometric designs and stylized floral motifs.

The Peshawbestown Road

These postcards from about 1915 show the old M-22, at that time called the Peshawbestown Road, that connected Peshawbestown with Suttons Bay. The "pony express" service carried mail and goods between the two settlements.

The Pony Express

Traverse Lake Region

Between Pyramid Point and Sugar Loaf is a broad valley occupied by Traverse and Lime Lakes, which was known as the Traverse Lake Region. Traverse Lake (now called Little Traverse Lake) sported black bass, perch, and blue gills and had a reputation for excellent fishing. Two early resorts were established on its shores about 1910. Atkinson's Resort was located on the south shore in a big farmhouse with wide verandas shaded by trees. Viskochil's resort, the Che-ke-ne-bis Inn, was located at the east end of the lake. The Inn had a boat livery, fishing equipment, tennis courts, and croquet grounds. Other small resorts were established over the years, along with many summer homes.

Located at the west end of the Little Traverse Lake was Lund's Scenic Garden, a kind of outdoor gallery with folk-art renditions of the life of Christ painted on large wooden panels displayed in a woodland setting. Created by hard work and divine inspiration, and the Reverends E. K. and Orpha Lund opened the garden in 1948. By the early 1950s it had some 10,000 registered visitors each summer.

Sugar Loaf "Mountain" is the highest point in Leelanau County, with an elevation of just over 800 feet. From the summit of Sugar Loaf one can see Lime Lake, Little Traverse Lake, Bass Lake, Shell Lake, and Lake Michigan. In the late 1940s Sugar Loaf Winter Sports Club was established. The club featured a three-quarter mile long main ski slope, a slalom bowl, a beginners' area, and several tows. Under the supervision of Hans (Peppi) Teichner, internationally known skier, hundreds of people, including students at the nearby Leelanau schools, learned to ski at Sugar Loaf.

Che-ke-ne-bis Lodge

TRAVERSE LAKE

Gamy Small Mouth Black Bass Fishing.

Newly built, specially arranged for Summer Guests and Anglers. Good, easy-rowing, comfortable boats. Good Cuisine, excellent service, thorough knowledge of the Fishing Grounds.

American Plan. $1.50-$2 per day. $8-$12 per week.

Address, FRANK VISKOCHIL, Maple City, Mich.

31

ADVERTISEMENT— CHE-KE-NE-BIS LODGE

— Grand Traverse, The Summer Land, 1910

Che-ke-ne-bis Inn
Maple City, Mich. R1

"Atkinsons" Traverse Lake, Maple City, Mich.

"Atkinsons," Traverse Lake

Traverse Lake, not far from Lake Leelanau, is a pretty lake set among great hills, with a big reputation for its black bass fishing. The initiated are sure to return each season for the scenery, the quiet, restful atmosphere and congenial company. There are two resorts, Atkinson's, noted for its generous hospitality, and Viskochil's, new last season, but already in the front ranks of popularity, due to the excellent service rendered. The table is appetizingly set with the best the countryside affords. The rooms are pleasant and airy.

There is a boat livery with excellent, easy rowing, comfortable boats, tennis courts, croquet grounds, etc. Mr. Viskochil has made the pleasure and comfort of his guests a study, and has been well rewarded.

He knows the lake well, and his fishing parties bring home generous strings. The scenery around the lake is beautiful. There are a number of trout streams, affording variety in piscatorial pursuits.

Traverse Lake is reached from Bodus on the Manistee and Northeastern, by carriage, or from Provemont. The trip offers much to the angler."

— Grand Traverse, the Summer Land, 1910

229

Traverse Lake Changes Hands

On the shores of Traverse Lake, almost in the shadow of Sugar Loaf Mountain, the highest point in northern Michigan, is Traverse Lake Resort. This quiet, comfortable resting place has long been a gathering place of those who want a vacation for a reasonable amount of money.

Under new management this year, and just reconditioned and remodeled, Traverse Lake Resort offers cool, clean rooms, an excellent dining room service, swimming, fishing for bass, perch and pickerel in the brilliant blue waters of Traverse Lake, and other recreational facilities. The management prides itself in furnishing soft beds, in clean, well-lighted rooms, and with modern conveniences of every sort.

Traverse Lake Resort is this year under the management of Mr. and Mrs. George Kelderhouse, and the resort is situated on highway M-22, just north of Glen Arbor, in Leelanau County.

— Traverse City Record Eagle, June 30, 1937

Lund's Scenic Garden — ANNUNCIATION

Lund's Scenic Garden: *at the west end of Little Traverse Lake is an amazing scenic wonderland. Among the trees, Rev. and Mrs. Lund have built a "Paradise in the Woods." Life size original oil paintings depicting the life of Christ, his death and resurrection have been placed at intervals. Escorted tours along the woodland paths with explanations of the scenes and scriptural references.*

— M-22 "The Manitou Trail," circa 1955

Lime Lake from Sugar Loaf

This extremely interesting mountain-like hill is officially recorded as being the highest point in lower Michigan.

Its elevation is a trifle over 800 feet, and it gets its name from the fact that its pinnacle is shaped like a loaf of sugar. It particularly takes this form in winter, when it is covered with glistening snow.

It is located on M-22, near Port Oneida, and is easily accessible for those desiring to make the climb, for there is a well traveled foot path leading from its base to the top.

The view from Mt. Sugar Loaf is wide and expansive and takes in some of the most beautiful and scenic countryside of Leelanau County.

From Mt. Sugar Loaf one can see Lime Lake, Traverse Lake, Bass Lake, Shell Lake, and Lake Michigan. These lakes are all perfect gems of beauty, with sandy beaches and heavily wooded shores. In the waters of these lakes, some of the best fishing in Michigan is to be had.

Towering above the blue waters of Lake Michigan, North and South Manitou Islands and the Fox Islands can be seen. On a clear day the much farther away Beaver Islands are plainly discernable, and nearer by, beautiful Pyramid Point, on the shores of Lake Michigan.

Mt. Sugar Loaf is well worth the climb on any clear day, and the view from its lofty height will always remain a cherished memory of Leelanau County.

— "Vacation Handbook and Fisherman's Guide, Leelanau County," *Leelanau Enterprise*, 1938

Winter Sports at Sugar Loaf

Winter Sports…One of the newer developments in Leelanau County but one which is significant and important, is Sugar Loaf, the winter sports club in the west central portion of the county. Carved from the virgin forests of a huge hill known as Sugar Loaf, are exciting ski runs and in the first year of its existence this club was selected for the down hill runs of the Central Ski Association with dozens of entries from half a dozen Midwestern states. A ski professional is engaged and a ski-tow has been installed. Plans are now under way to greatly expand this winter sports center by adding toboggan slides, skating rinks and other facilities for outdoor winter recreation. Already the Sugar Loaf club has caught the fancy of outdoor enthusiasts from Chicago and Detroit and soon special ski trains will be bringing these people to Leelanau County for their winter vacations. Sugar Loaf seems destined to become one of the mid-west's important winter sport centers.

— *Vacation Days in the Grand Traverse Bay Region*
Traverse City Area Chamber of Commerce, circa 1949

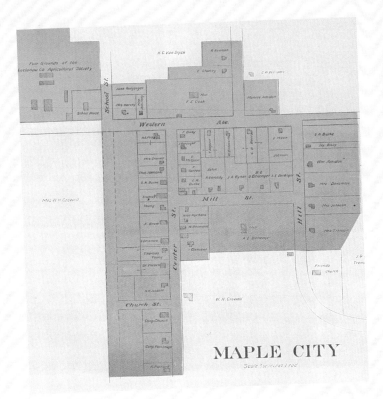

MAPLE CITY

MAP OF MAPLE CITY, *Atlas of Leelanau County*, 1900
Maple City is located 14 miles south of Leland, and
seven miles from Solon. In 1900 it had a population
of 125. Twice-daily stages went to Solon and Glen
Haven. Congregational and Friends churches served the
community. The busy village had a saw and planing
mill, a carpenter, a blacksmith, two hardware stores,
two dressmakers, a milliner, a general store, a grocer,
a butcher, and a creamery. It also had a lawyer, a
physician, a furniture maker, and an undertaker.

HOTEL DENSMORE,
E.F. Densmore, Prop.
MAPLE CITY, -MICH.

————

Close attention given the traveling
public. Connections made with all
passenger trains at Solon.
Traveling salesmen driven anywhere
in the County at reasonable rates.

—

Advertisement from *Leelanau Enterprise*,
January 13, 1898

Maple City

Maple City was first settled in 1866 by J.T. Sturtevant and his son, who built a factory that made wooden shoe pegs. It was originally called Peg Town, but changed to Maple City when its post office was established. A small hotel and sawmill were built. The mill was later sold and converted to the production of wooden bowls, handles for brooms and pitchforks, shingles, and wooden flooring. The peg factory operated until 1880 when it burned. The mill produced wooden goods until 1916. Maple City maintains the charms of a quaint village.

We are now drinking Milwaukee Beer also good old Strohs.   — E.K.

Postmarked Maple City, 1939 / Mailed to Detroit, Michigan

Dear friend Emily —

We sure are having hot weather here and I suppose it's the same there. Took in the Cherry Festival in T.C. and it was good and the fireworks also in the evening. Didn't have a strawberry this summer as they all froze and it hurt the cherry too. (Write soon)   — Love from Marion

Postmarked Maple City, 1949 / Mailed to Tacoma, Washington

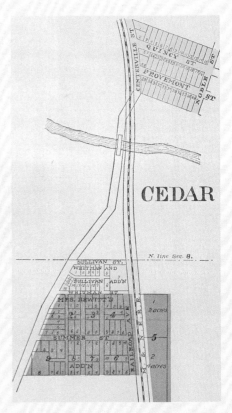

Cedar

Cedar was already a small community when a branch of the Manistee and Northeastern Railroad came through about 1899. It originally had been called Cedar City, but the name was shortened to Cedar. The name was chosen because of the vast growth of cedar in the vicinity. The Sullivan Lumber Company erected a shingle mill and shortly after, the Dewey Stave Company built a mill to manufacture barrel staves and hoops. The

population of the village peaked in about 1900 with 600 inhabitants. It had two general stores, a bank, a hotel, a shoe store, a Congregational Church, and a Friends Church. When the mill closed in 1912 and the factory in 1916, farming became the main occupation. Cedar once had a predominantly Polish population and annually holds a Polka Festival in July.

Above: Cedar's Center of Much Trade

Cedar, Michigan, located thirteen miles from Traverse City on Leelanau County highway 611 is a marketing and trading center for several townships. Lake Leelanau and Traverse Lake resorters of the vicinity make it their headquarters.

Back in 1895 the village became actively engaged in lumbering. There were four mills busily occupied in sending out cedar logs and finished lumber. By 1910 however, the lumbering decreased and the community turned to farming for a livelihood. In recent years farming and resorting have been the source of business for the dozen or so merchants of the community.

— Traverse City Record Eagle, June 30, 1935

Right: Map of Cedar, *Atlas of Leelanau County*, 1900

Cedar is located 16 miles south of Leland and 12 miles northwest of Traverse City. It was a stop on the Manistee and Northeastern Railroad. In 1900 Cedar had a population of 600. Congregational and Friends churches served the community. Cedar had a lumber and shingle mill, a barrel stave company, two general stores, two druggists, and a confectionery. By 1903 it had two saloons, a shoemaker, a livery, and two blacksmiths were added to the community.

Right: Cedar, which was founded about 1885 by Benjamin Boughey, was one of the later towns founded in Leelanau County. It was originally called Cedar City.

Greilickville

Greilickville is located in the southeastern section of Leelanau County, three miles north of Traverse City. It was originally called Norrisville after Seth and Albert Norris who settled there in 1852 and built a gristmill, brickyard, and tavern. A few years later Godfrey Greilick came from Austria with his five sons and built a water-powered sawmill. In 1862 the Greilick brothers built another sawmill, a dock, and a brewery. The settlement took the name Greilickville in 1903 when the Traverse City, Leelanau and Manistique Railroad came through. The Traverse Beach Summer Resort was located just north of Greilickville and was one of the finest resorts in the area.

Other Settlements

There were many other settlements in Leelanau County that are not represented in this book. Two early Native American settlements were Ahgostatown and Onumeneseville. Many early villages were dependent on the timber industry and are now ghost towns. Among these are Gill's Pier, North Unity, Good Harbor, and Port Oneida. Some settlements were dependent on the railroad and died out when railroad service was discontinued. These include Hatch's Crossing, Keswick, Solon, and Schomberg. Other settlements were primarily farming communities and even had their own post offices. Among these were Miller Hill, Shetland, and Isadore. The North and South Fox Islands saw farming and logging operations, a government lighthouse, and failed attempts for a summer resort.

Right: The Traverse Beach Summer Resort, located just north of Greilickville, was proclaimed to be one of the finest in the Midwest. The grounds, exceeding a hundred acres, were situated between Grand Traverse Bay and a small, picturesque lake known as Cedar Lake. The hotel was located on a gradual slope, about 300 feet from the sandy beach, and commanded a fine view of the bay. The hotel was finely furnished and could accommodate 100 guests. Besides fishing and bathing, the hotel offered shaded croquet, lawn tennis courts, and a bowling alley. Livery service was available for scenic drives in the area. Financial hard times fell upon the owners and the resort changed hands several times. For a while it was known as the "Baptist Resort" because of the religious affiliation of the owners.

Weather is fine here but
we'll have to go home soon.
Otto wants to stay
a thousand weeks.

— Rose —

Postmarked Maple City, 1915
Mailed to Chicago, Illinois

The End

The Authors

Christine and Tom had each been vacationing in Leelanau County for about ten years before they met in Grand Rapids. Soon they realized that they both vacationed on the east side of Glen Lake – Christine at Scotty's Haven and Tom at Glenview Resort, less than a mile apart. They share a love of the area and a fascination with its history. Their collection of antique postcards was the inspiration for their book, *Vintage Views of Leelanau County*.

Tom is a native of Grand Rapids but has traveled extensively throughout Michigan. He attended Grand Valley State University and is a life-long student of history. He has held various positions with Sears in his 34-year career, and is currently an executive with Sears Home Services. Tom is an avid postcard collector focusing on Michigan real photo cards.

Christine is also a native of Grand Rapids where she is the librarian for Local Historical Collections at the Grand Rapids Public Library. She was previously a bookseller for 22 years, working in several bookstores in Grand Rapids and later as a district manager for Community Newscenters. For a few years Christine had her own note card business, *Vintage Views*, which were reproductions of antique Michigan postcards. Christine has an undergraduate degree from Aquinas College and a Master's in Library Science from Western Michigan University. She is an avid reader of Michigan history and collects old Michigan travel and tourist memorabilia.

Christine and Tom are active members in the West Michigan Post Card Club. They are also members of the Leelanau Historical Society, the Grand Traverse Pioneer and Historical Society, and the Grand Rapids Historical Society. Christine and Tom live with their dog Max in a 1912 Arts and Craft bungalow in East Grand Rapids. They have a small cottage on Glen Lake where they spend as much time as possible.

Bibliography and Sources Cited

Books, Pamphlets, and Brochures

*Atlas of Leelanau County, Michigan. Philadelphia: C.O. Titus, 1881.

*Atlas of Leelanau County, Michigan. Knoxville, TN.: Charles E. Ferris, 1900.

*Beauty Spots in Leelanau, 1901 Souvenir. Northport: W.E. Campbell, 1901.

*Bennett, James O'Donell. West Michigan's Flaming Forests. Grand Rapids: West Michigan Tourist Association, 1935.

*Carefree Days in West Michigan. [Grand Rapids]: West Michigan Tourist Association, 1940-1966.

*Cedar Lodge, Northport Point, Mich. [Northport: Geo. C. Anderson], circa 1930.

*Cold Springs Inn on Beautiful Glen Lake. Grand Rapids: Etheridge, circa 1920.

Crowner, Gerald R. The South Manitou Story. Mio, MI: Futura Printing, 1982.

Dalton, Elmer L. A Brief History of Leelanau County, Michigan. Leland: Leelanau County Clerk's Office, 1924.

*Day, D.H. [David Henry]. Glen Lake Region. Traverse City: Herald and Record Co., 1911.

*Day Forest Estates on Beautiful Glen Lake. [n.p.: Day Forests Estates], circa 1928.

Dickinson, Julia Terry. The Story of Leelanau. Omena: Solle's Bookshop, 1951.

Empire History Notes. Empire: Empire Township Heritage Group, 1973.

*Fountain Point House and Cottages. Traverse City: Ebner Brothers Printers, 1927.

*George Raff's Mackinaw Fishing Camp, Northport, Michigan. [Northport: George Raff], circa 1930.

*Glen Lake, Leelanau County, Michigan. Traverse City: L.R. Henderson, 1931.

*Grand Traverse Bay Region: Michigan's Sunshine Corner. Traverse City: Traverse City Area Chamber of Commerce, 1947.

*Grand Traverse Region. Traverse City: Herald and Record Co., circa 1914.

*Grand Traverse, The Summer Land. [Traverse City: Traverse City Board of Trade], 1910.

Haswell, Susan Olsen. A Garden Apart: An Agricultural and Settlement History of Michigan's Sleeping Bear Dunes National Lakeshore Region. Omaha: National Park Service, 1994.

History of Leelanau Township / By the Leelanau Township Historical Writers Group. [Leland: Friends of the Leelanau Township Library], circa 1982.

*Inglis, James Gale. Northern Michigan Handbook for Travelers. Petoskey: Geo. E. Sprang, 1898.

Johnson, A.H., Company, Michigan, Leelanau County: Historical and Descriptive. [Traverse City: Traverse Bay Eagle Job Office], 1880.

Johnson, Charles F. A History of Old Settlements from Leelanau County. [Grand Rapids: Charles F. Johnson], circa 1995.

Kalt, Brian C. Sixties Sandstorm: The Fight over the Establishment of a Sleeping Bear National Lakeshore, 1961 - 1970. East Lansing: Michigan State University Press, 2001.

Karamanski, Theodore J. A Nationalized Lakeshore: The Creation and Administration of Sleeping Bear Dunes National Lakeshore. Omaha: U.S. Dept. of the Interior, National Park Service, 2000.

Kasson Township Heritage Group. Remembering Yesterday. [n.p.]: Kasson Heritage Group, circa 1976.

*King's Official Route Guide. Chicago: S.J. King, 1920.

Korn, Claire V. Michigan State Parks: Yesterday Through Tomorrow. East Lansing: Michigan State University Press, 1989.

*Leelanau Chamber of Commerce. Leelanau County, The Land of Delight. Grand Rapids: White Printing Co., 1926.

*Leelanau County, The Land of Delight. [Leland: Leelanau County Board of Supervisors], circa 1930.

*Leelanau Homestead: A Unit of the Leelanau Schools. [Glen Arbor: The Leelanau Homestead], circa 1957.

*Leelanau Lodge, on Delightful Lake Leelanau. [Lake Leelanau, Leelanau Lodge], circa 1946.

*The Leelanau, Omena, Michigan, Season of 1900. Ann Arbor: Athens Press, 1900.

*Leland as a Summer Resort. circa 1903. Reprint [Leland]: Leelanau Enterprise and Leelanau Historical Society, [n.p.].

*Leland Golf and Yacht Club, Resort Directory of Leland and Surrounding Region. Leland: Leelanau Enterprise, 1937.

*Leland Lodge, Michigan. [Leland: George C. Anderson], circa 1958.

Littell, Edmund M. 100 Years in Leelanau. Leland: The Print Shop, 1965.

Lund, Orpha. A History of Lund's Scenic Garden. [n.p.]:, circa 1965.

*M-22 "The Manitou Trail". [Frankfort, MI: M-22 Association], circa 1955.

MacDonald, Eric and Alanen, Arnold R. Tending a 'Comfortable Wilderness.' Omaha: U.S. Dept. of the Interior, National Park Service, 2000.

*McCracken, Lawrence. McCracken's 1940 Guide to Michigan. Pontiac: Lawrence McCracken, 1940.

*Michigan, A Guide to the Wolverine State. New York: Oxford University Press, 1941.

*Michigan, A Summer and Health Resort State. Lansing: R. Smith Printing Co., 1898.

*Michigan in Summer. [n.p.]: Grand Rapids and Indiana Railway. 1903, 1904, 1905, 1910.

*Michigan Scenic Highways: Around Lake Michigan Tour. Lansing: Magazine of Michigan, 1933.

*Michigan Transit Co., 1921. [Chicago: Michigan Transit Co.], 1921.

More Than a Century: Suttons Bay, Mich. [Suttons Bay]: Suttons Bay Chamber of Commerce, [1976].

*Northern Michigan Line, 1911. Chicago: Northern Michigan Transportation Co., 1911.

*Northport Beach Resort, Northport, Michigan [Northport: A.M. Leslie], 1902.

*The Oaks. [Omena: Mr. and Mrs. Louis A. Solem], circa 1922.

Old Settlers Picnic Association. A History of Old Settlers Picnics and Old Settlers. [n.p.: Old Settlers Picnic Association], 1999.

*Omena Resort. Grand Rapids, MI: Dickinson Bros. circa 1898, circa 1901, circa 1903.

*Page, Abel. Homes for All in Michigan. Grand Rapids: West Michigan Printing Co., 1892.

*Parks of the People. Lansing: Department of Conservation of Michigan, circa 1924.

*Peppler's on Beautiful Glen Lake. [Maple City: Bill and Helen Peppler], circa 1965.

*Phelps, William Henry. Ye Lakes and Hills of Michigan. Detroit: Michigan Christian Advocate Press, circa 1933.

*Powers, Perry. *A History of Northern Michigan and Its People*. Chicago: Lewis Publishing Co., 1912.

A Proposed Sleeping Bear National Seashore, Natural History Report. [n.p.]: U.S. Dept. of the Interior, National Park Service, 1961.

Rader, Robert Dwight. *Beautiful Glen Arbor Township*. Village Press, 1977.

Remembering Empire Through Pictures. Empire: Empire Township Heritage Group, 1978.

Road Map and Business Directory of Leelanau County. Leland: *Leelanau Enterprise*, circa 1925.

Robbins, Sabin. *100 Summers: Affectionate History of Northport Point*. Elk Rapids, MI: Bayshore Books, 1999.

Ruchhoft, R.H. *Exploring North Manitou, South Manitou, High and Garden Islands of the Lake Michigan Archipelago*. Cincinnati: Pucelle Press, 1991.

Rusco, Rita Hadra. *North Manitou Island: Between Sunrise and Sunset*. [n.p.]: R.H. Rusco, circa 1991.

Six Drives Out of Many Delightful Drives in the Immediate Vicinity of Traverse City. [Traverse City: Chamber of Commerce], circa 1935.

Sleeping Bear Dunesmobile Scenic Rides. [Glen Haven: Marion and Louis Warnes], circa 1959.

Some Other Day: Remembering Empire, 2nd ed. Empire: The Empire Area Heritage Group, 1987.

*Sprague, Elvin L. *Sprague's History of Grand Traverse and Leelanau Counties*. [Indianapolis]: B.F. Bowen, 1903.

*Sprague, Elvin. *The Traverse Region: Historical and Descriptive*. Chicago: H.R. Page & Co., 1884.

State Parks of Michigan: A Report of the Past, A Look to the Future. [Lansing]: Michigan Dept. of Conservation, 1957.

Stocking, Kathleen. *Letters from the Leelanau*. Ann Arbor: University of Michigan Press, circa 1990.

Stroup, Donald. *The Manistee & Northeastern: The Life and Death of a Railroad*. Kalamazoo: Historical Society of Michigan, 1964.

Stuart, Augusta. *Northport Point*, Michigan. Lenmore Press, 1970.

Suttons Bay, Leelanau County, Michigan. [Suttons Bay: Chamber of Commerce], 1954.

*Thompson, J. Russell. *J. Russell Thompson's Resort Guide 1907*. Grand Rapids: Etheridge Printing, 1907.

Vacation at Northport and Leelanau Township, The Tip of the Little Finger of Michigan. [n.p. : n.p.], circa 1940.

Vacation Days in Michigan's Grand Traverse Bay Region. [Traverse City: Traverse City Area Chamber of Commerce], 1948 - 1966.

Vacation Handbook and Fisherman's Guide, Leelanau County. Leland: *Leelanau Enterprise*, 1938 - 1942.

Vent, Myron H. *South Manitou Island: From Pioneer Settlemetn to National Park*. New York: Publishing Center for Cultural Resources, 1973.

Vent, Myron H. and Vent, William E. *Pioneer and Other Stories of South Manitou Island*. Aurora, IL: J.W. Reproductions, 1990.

*Wait, S.E. and Anderson, Comp. *Old Settlers: A Historical and Chronological Record*. Traverse City: Ebner Brothers, 1918.

Wakefield, Lawrence. *Leelanau County Postcard History*. [n.p.]: Leelanau County Historical Society, circa 1992.

Wakefield, Lawrence. *Sail & Rail: A Narrative History of Transportation in Western Michigan*. Holt, MI: Thunder Bay Press, 1996.

Waterman, Warren Gookin. *Forest and Dunes, From Point Betsie to Sleeping Bear*. Evanston, IL: Northwestern University, circa 1922.

Weeks, George. *Mem-Ka-Weh: Dawning of the Grand Traverse Band of Ottawa and Chippewa Indians*. [n.p.]: Grand Traverse Band of Ottawa and Chippewa Indians, 1992.

Weeks, George. *Sleeping Bear: Its Lore, Legends and First People*. Glen Arbor: Cottage Book Shop of Glen Arbor and the Historical Society of Michigan, circa 1988.

Weeks, George. *Sleeping Bear: Yesterday and Tomorrow*. Franklin, MI: Altwerger and Mandel Publishing, 1990.

West Michigan Pike, [Muskegon]: West Michigan Pike Association, 1914, 1915.

West Michigan Vacation Directory. Grand Rapids: West Michigan Tourist Association, 1929.

Western Michigan: The Land of Opportunity. [n.p.]: Western Michigan Development Bureau, circa 1909.

* Winchell, Alexander. *Grand Traverse Region, A Report on the Geological and Industrial Resources*. Ann Arbor: Dr. Chase's Steam Printing House, 1866.

Wood, Guy, Company. *Bibliography of Leelanauiania*. Empire: [n.p.]: 1981.

Newspapers

Grand Rapids Press. 1901, 1926.
Leelanau Enterprise and Tribune. 1898 1954.
Traverse City Record Eagle. 1922-1942.

Special Collections

*Richmond, Rebecca. Unpublished Diaries from the Richmond Family Papers, Local Historical Collections, Grand Rapids Public Library.

*Stace, Arthur W. Writings of Arthur W. Stace. West Michigan Tourist Association Collection. State Archives of Michigan.

*Indicates Source Cited

Credits

9 *(left)* Leelanau Historical Museum, *(right)* Traverse City Area Chamber of Commerce, 11 Leelanau Historical Museum, 12 Grand Rapids Public Library, Local Historical Collections, 13 *(left) Leelanau Enterprise*, 15 *(top)* Empire Area Museum, 16 *(left)* Leelanau Historical Museum, *(right) Leelanau Enterprise*, 19 *(right)* Grand Rapids Public Library, Local Historical Collections, 21 Empire Area Museum, 24 Bentley Historical Library, University of Michigan, 25 Grand Traverse Pioneer and Historical Society, 26 *(bottom left & right)* James Winslow Collection, 27 *(top)* James Winslow Collection, *(bottom)* Leelanau Historical Museum, 28 *(top)* Jerry Conroy Collection, 29 Stanley Kufta Collection, State Archives of Michigan, 30 Ralph Russell Tinkham photograph series, Bentley Historical Library, University of Michigan 31 *(bottom)* Leelanau Historical Museum, 32 Leelanau County Road Commission, 33 Empire Area Museum, 34 Leelanau Historical Museum, 35 *(bottom)* West Michigan Tourist Association, 36 *(bottom)* Traverse City Area Chamber of Commerce, 37 *(center)* West Michigan Tourist Association, *(bottom)* Curt Teich Postcard Archives, Lake County (IL) Discovery Museum 39 Leelanau Historical Museum, 41 *(top)* Empire Area Museum, 42 *(top)* Empire Area Museum, 45 *(bottom)* Jerry Conroy Collection, 50 *(top)* Curt Teich Postcard Archives, Lake County (IL) Discovery Museum 51 State Archives of Michigan, 52-53 Grand Rapids Public Library, Local Historical Collections, 56 *(top)* Phil Balyeat Photograph, *(bottom)* Grand Rapids Public Library, Local Historical Collections, 57 Phil Balyeat Photograph, 58-59 Grand Rapids Public Library, Local Historical Collections, 61 *(top)* State Archives of Michigan, *(bottom)* Phil Balyeat Photograph, 62 Phil Balyeat Photograph, 63 Avery Color Studios, 64 Jerry Conroy Collection, 65 Leelanau Historical Museum, 66 Jerry Conroy Collection, 70 Claude Thomas Stoner photograph series, Bentley Historical Library, University of Michigan 73 George Weeks Collection, 74 *(top)* State Archives of Michigan, 75 *(bottom)* Leelanau Historical Museum, 78 Sleeping Bear Dunes National Lakeshore, 80 *(top)* Empire Area Museum, 83 Empire Area Museum, 86 *(top)* Curt Teich Postcard Archives, Lake County (IL) Discovery Museum 87 *(top)* Grand Traverse Pioneer and Historical Society, 88 *(top)* Curt Teich Postcard Archives, Lake County (IL) Discovery Museum *(bottom)* Avery Color Studio, 89 Empire Area Museum, 90 *(bottom)* Empire Area Museum, 94 *(top)* Empire Area Museum, 97 Empire Area Museum, 102 *(top)* Leelanau Historical Museum, *(bottom)* Jerry Conroy Collection, 103 Ralph Russell Tinkham photograph series, Bentley Historical Library, University of Michigan, 106 Leelanau Historical Museum, 107 Jerry Conroy Collection, 113 George Weeks Collection, 114 Leelanau Historical Museum, 116 *(top)* Jerry Conroy Collection, 117 *(top)* Sylvan Inn, 118 *(bottom)* Glen Arbor History Group, 123 *(top)* Empire Area Museum, *(bottom)* Homestead Collection, 124 *(top left & bottom)* Homestead Collection, 125 *(right)* Avery Color Studio, 127 Fountain Point, 129 *(top left & bottom left)* Leelanau Historical Museum, 130 Leelanau Historical Museum, 131 *(top)* Leelanau Historical Museum, 132 Grand Traverse Pioneer and Historical Society, 133 *(bottom)* Jerry Conroy Collection, 134 Jerry Conroy Collection, 137 Grand Traverse Pioneer and Historical Society, 140 Leelanau Historical Museum, 141 *(bottom)* Leelanau Historical Museum, 152 Leelanau Historical Museum, 153 *(top)* Grand Traverse Pioneer and Historical Society, *(bottom)* Leelanau Historical Museum, 154 Grand Traverse Pioneer and Historical Society, 157 Grand Traverse Lighthouse Foundation, 160 Leelanau Historical Museum, 162 *(bottom)* Jerry Conroy Collection, 163 *(top)* Jerry Conroy Collection, 164 *(bottom)* Stanley Kufta Collection, State Archives of Michigan, 165 Stanley Kufta Collection, State Archives of Michigan, 167 *(top)* Stanley Kufta Collection, State Archives of Michigan, 171-172 Leelanau Historical Museum, 173 *(top)* Leelanau Historical Museum, 178 *(top)* Leelanau Historical Museum, 179 *(top)* Leelanau Historical Museum, *(bottom)* Jerry Conroy Collection, 181 *(top)* Grand Traverse Pioneer and Historical Society, *(bottom)* Leelanau Historical Museum, 184 *(top)* Betty Armstrong postcard collection, Bentley Historical Library, University of Michigan *(bottom)* Leelanau Historical Museum, 188 Leelanau Historical Museum, 191 *(right)* Grand Traverse Pioneer and Historical Society, 192 Leelanau Historical Museum, 195 *(top)* from the brochure "Omena Resort," Bentley Historical Library, University of Michigan, *(bottom)* Leelanau Historical Museum, 198 Leelanau Historical Museum, 200 *(top)* Leelanau Historical Museum, 201 *(top)* Leelanau Historical Museum, 202 *(bottom)* Claude Thomas Stoner photograph series, Bentley Historical Library, University of Michigan, 203 *(bottom)* Jerry Conroy Collection, 207 Randa Fredrickson photograph series, Bentley Historical Library, University of Michigan, 208 *(bottom)* Leelanau Historical Museum, 209 *(top)* Leelanau Historical Museum, *(bottom)* Steve Truman, 210 *(top)* Postcard collection, Bentley Historical Library, University of Michigan, *(bottom)* Empire Area Museum, 211 *(top)* Ethel Paulina Furst Stormer, *(bottom)* Postcard collection, Bentley Historical Library, University of Michigan, 212 *(top)* Leelanau Historical Museum, *(bottom)* Ethel Paulina Furst Stormer, 213 *(top)* Empire Area Museum, *(bottom)* Leelanau Historical Museum, 214 *(top left)* Grand Traverse Pioneer and Historical Society, *(bottom)* Leelanau Historical Museum, 215 Empire Area Museum, 216 Leelanau Historical Museum, 217 *(top)* Ethel Paulina Furst Stormer, *(bottom)* Randa Fredrickson photograph series, Bentley Historical Library, University of Michigan, 220-221 Leelanau Historical Museum, 222 *(top)* Grand Traverse Pioneer and Historical Society, *(bottom)* Ethel Paulina Furst Stormer, 223 *(top)* Leelanau Historical Museum, *(bottom)* Sleeping Bear Dunes National Lakeshore, 224 *(top)* Grand Rapids Public Library, Local Historical Collections, *(bottom)* Leelanau Historical Museum, 225 *(left)* Omena Presbyterian Church photograph series, Bentley Historical Library, University of Michigan, (right) Grand Rapids Public Library, Local Historical Collections, 226 *(top)* Omena Presbyterian Church photograph series, Bentley Historical Library, University of Michigan, *(bottom)* Leelanau Historical Museum, 227 Leelanau Historical Museum, 228 Empire Area Collection, 231 *(bottom)* Grand Traverse Pioneer and Historical Society, 232 *(top)* Leelanau Historical Collection, *(bottom)* Jerry Conroy Collection, 233 *(bottom)* Stanley Kufta Collection, State Archives of Michigan, 234 *(center left)* Grand Traverse Pioneer and Historical Society, *(bottom)* Leelanau Historical Museum, 235 *(bottom)* Grand Traverse Pioneer and Historical Society

All other postcards and memorabilia from the authors' collection. The publisher will be pleased to rectify any photography copyright ommissions or inaccuracies in future printings.